THE MILITARY PAY MUDDLE

MARTIN BINKIN

THE MILITARY PAY MUDDLE

THE BROOKINGS INSTITUTION

Washington, D.C.

Copyright © 1975 by
THE BROOKINGS INSTITUTION
1775 Massachusetts Avenue, N.W., Washington, D.C. 20036

Library of Congress Cataloging in Publication Data:
Binkin, Martin, 1928–
  The military pay muddle.
  (Studies in defense policy)
  Includes bibliographical references.
  1. United States—Armed Forces—Pay, allowances, etc.
I. Title.   II. Series.
UC74.B56   355.1'35   75-4422
ISBN 0-8157-0961-7

9 8 7 6 5 4 3 2 1

THE BROOKINGS INSTITUTION is an independent organization devoted to nonpartisan research, education, and publication in economics, government, foreign policy, and the social sciences generally. Its principal purposes are to aid in the development of sound public policies and to promote public understanding of issues of national importance.

The Institution was founded on December 8, 1927, to merge the activities of the Institute for Government Research, founded in 1916, the Institute of Economics, founded in 1922, and the Robert Brookings Graduate School of Economics and Government, founded in 1924.

The Board of Trustees is responsible for the general administration of the Institution, while the immediate direction of the policies, program, and staff is vested in the President, assisted by an advisory committee of the officers and staff. The by-laws of the Institution state: "It is the function of the Trustees to make possible the conduct of scientific research, and publication, under the most favorable conditions, and to safeguard the independence of the research staff in the pursuit of their studies and in the publication of the results of such studies. It is not a part of their function to determine, control, or influence the conduct of particular investigations or the conclusions reached."

The President bears final responsibility for the decision to publish a manuscript as a Brookings book. In reaching his judgment on the competence, accuracy, and objectivity of each study, the President is advised by the director of the appropriate research program and weighs the views of a panel of expert outside readers who report to him in confidence on the quality of the work. Publication of a work signifies that it is deemed a competent treatment worthy of public consideration but does not imply endorsement of conclusions or recommendations.

The Institution maintains its position of neutrality on issues of public policy in order to safeguard the intellectual freedom of the staff. Hence interpretations or conclusions in Brookings publications should be understood to be solely those of the authors and should not be attributed to the Institution, to its trustees, officers, or other staff members, or to the organizations that support its research.

FOREWORD

The rising cost of defense manpower has profoundly affected the size and character of recent defense budgets. One of the principal factors contributing to this trend has been the marked increase in the military payroll. While military manpower was reduced by 1.3 million between fiscal years 1968 and 1975, the military payroll went up by over $6 billion. Since 1968, average military pay has more than doubled.

Martin Binkin argues here that the United States is not getting the best value for this increased expenditure. His assessment of the armed forces pay structure reveals a system, perhaps appropriate for a military establishment of an earlier era, that has become a costly anachronism. He contends that those already in the services as well as lawmakers and prospective volunteers are often unaware of the full value of military compensation simply because some of its elements are not easily perceived or understood. Moreover, because its underlying rationale calls for paying people partly on the basis of their "needs" rather than exclusively for their contribution to national security, the system in some instances attracts those who are costly in relation to their skills. As a result, the United States is paying more than is necessary to field its present military forces; alternatively, the nation could obtain more effective forces without increasing current levels of defense spending.

To reverse this trend, the author makes three basic recommendations: paying salaries to military personnel according to the principle of equal pay for equal work; making the military retirement system more nearly parallel with the federal civilian retirement system; and revising the dependent health care program. These measures are designed to overhaul a paternalistic system (justifiable when military pay was inordinately low) so as to make it more responsive to market forces.

Martin Binkin, a senior fellow in the Brookings Foreign Policy Studies program, is the author of two previous Brookings studies in defense policy: *Support Costs in the Defense Budget: The Submerged One-Third* (1972) and *U.S. Reserve Forces: The Problem of the Weekend Warrior* (1974). He is also coauthor of *All-Volunteer Armed Forces: Progress, Problems, and Prospects,* a study published in 1973 by the Senate Armed Services Committee.

The Institution thanks General Charles L. Bolté, Philip Odeen, and R. James Woolsey for their helpful comments on the manuscript. During the course of the study, the author received useful data and assistance from numerous officials in the Department of Defense to whom he is indebted. He also benefited greatly from the comments of many people on earlier drafts of the manuscript and especially thanks Stephen Herbits, John Pronsky, and Francis W. White. Among his Brookings colleagues, he is grateful to Edward R. Fried for wise counsel and encouragement and to Henry J. Aaron, Barry M. Blechman, Herman Gilster, Jerry Kotchka, Henry Owen, and Alton H. Quanbeck for valuable suggestions. Tadd Fisher edited the manuscript and Christine Lipsey typed it.

The Institution acknowledges the assistance of the Ford Foundation, whose grant helps to support its work in defense studies. The views expressed herein are those of the author and should not be ascribed to the persons who provided data or who commented on the manuscript, to the Ford Foundation, or to the trustees, officers, or other staff members of the Brookings Institution.

KERMIT GORDON
President

Washington, D.C.
April 1975

CONTENTS

Tables

CHAPTER ONE

INTRODUCTION

Over the past decade, the United States has been paying progressively more to field its military forces. One of the most important contributing factors has been the sharp rise in the cost of defense manpower, a matter of considerable concern both to critics of high defense spending and to those who are fearful of the national security implications that might attend an inordinate investment in manpower at the expense of weapon systems.

In the main, the growth of manpower costs can be charged to two factors:

First, reductions in the number of defense employees have not kept pace with reductions in combat forces (divisions, ships, aircraft). Thus, more people are being used to acquire, operate, direct, and sustain each combat unit than were required a decade ago. This structural change has resulted mainly from changes in technology and organization but also from the large support infrastructure inherited from the Vietnam war.

Second, the price of defense manpower has been increasing dramatically since 1968; indeed, military pay increases have been a major cause of changes in recent defense budgets. This trend, which began in the interest of equity and was sustained by the need to underwrite the transition to an all-volunteer service, has resulted in more than a two-fold increase in average per capita military pay between fiscal years 1968 and 1976.

For these reasons, the efficiency with which defense manpower is used has attracted a large share of attention, and the Department of Defense is currently emphasizing improvements in the ratio of personnel employed in combat jobs to those in support jobs. The price of defense manpower, on the other hand, has been subjected to less scrutiny. This

1

study concentrates on one aspect of the price of defense manpower—the military compensation system. Its main purpose is not to judge whether military pay is too high or too low, or whether it is comparable to civilian pay, but whether the present incentive structure encourages the most efficient use of military manpower.

The present system of pay and allowances is the legacy of the small, relatively unskilled cadre-type combat forces that characterized the American military during most of its history before Pearl Harbor. Cash pay was extremely low, but practically everyone in the military, the large majority of whom were single, was provided free food, uniforms, and accommodations. Cash allowances were rare exceptions. For many service people, the commissaries and exchanges provided the only available shopping sources since most military installations were located outside metropolitan areas. Because a substantial number of the personnel were career-minded, turnover was small. The resultant limited opportunities for promotion were offset in part by "fogies"—periodic increases in basic pay based on years served. The prospect of a retirement pension constituted the principal fringe benefit for military personnel, many of whom served full careers.[1]

The abrupt changes in the size, composition, and technology of military forces brought on by U.S. involvement in World War II and sustained for three decades by U.S. cold war strategy have had important implications for the military pay system. In sharp contrast to the prewar period, the military services today are composed of a large proportion of young noncareer personnel expected to serve only one term of enlistment; this proportion ranges from about 75 percent in the Marine Corps to 49 percent in the Air Force. More than half of all military personnel are now married, and those married have, on average, about three dependents. Twenty-seven percent of the enlisted personnel's skills in 1941 were classified as technical, scientific, or mechanical; 50 percent were so classified in 1974. Furthermore, since the end of the draft, a recruitment system based on market forces has been replacing a system in which heavy reliance on conscription resulted in the underpayment of personnel.

1. Before 1935 a minimum of thirty years of service was required for retirement. In 1935, to reduce the World War I "hump"—the cluster of people who had entered the services during the war years—voluntary retirement of army officers with as little as fifteen years of service was authorized. Since shortly after World War II, voluntary retirement has been permitted after twenty years of service.

To keep pace with these changes, military pay has been increased and by most accounts has now reached comparability with federal civilian pay; moreover, it is now sufficiently competitive to attract the required number of volunteers from the civilian labor force. At the same time, the cost of providing fringe benefits has increased; indeed, the burgeoning costs of retirement and health care programs, the principal fringe benefits, have levied a heavy toll on the defense budget. If the present course is continued, these two programs—which in themselves accounted for over $9 billion, or about 10 percent of total defense spending in fiscal year 1975—will probably consume a growing proportion of the total budget for military manpower. Hence, the need to assess the military pay system, which is the principal determinant of the price of military manpower, is all the more pressing.

CHAPTER TWO

THE STRUCTURE OF MILITARY PAY

To most workers, take-home pay—the amount of their paycheck after deductions—constitutes the most visible yardstick of their earnings. Such payments, however, unsatisfactorily measure how much a person receives for his labor. To an increasing extent, in addition to their salary or wages, American workers are being provided benefits to which they attach significance and which represent important and measurable expenditures to employers. The proliferation of perquisites and fringe benefits over the past several decades has increased the economic well-being of the American worker but at the same time has made it more difficult for him to answer the question "How much do I earn?" These trends are particularly evident in the military establishment, whose compensation system over the years has evolved into a complex assortment of pay, allowances, and benefits.

Basic Pay and Allowances

Basic pay, the only cash element to which *all* military personnel are entitled, is best defined as compensation for work performed. By tradition, military rank has been the acceptable proxy for skill and responsibility; hence basic pay rates are tied to rank. Moreover, within each rank, basic pay varies depending on the number of accumulated years of military service. Effective October 1974, monthly basic pay ranged from $344.10 for a new recruit to $3,000 for a general officer with at least sixteen years of service.

The provision of food and shelter, in addition to basic pay, is based on precedent dating back to the Continental Army. When these necessities are furnished by the government, cash does not change hands; "free" goods and services are received. When food or housing is not provided in kind, either because facilities are unavailable or because of individual preference, military personnel are paid cash allowances intended to defray the expense of obtaining food and housing from the private economy. Cash "quarters allowances," based on rank and dependency status, range from $63.30 a month for an unmarried recruit to $303.90 a month for a general officer with dependents. About half of all military personnel receive cash quarters allowances. Cash "subsistence allowances" for enlisted personnel are now $2.41 a day. Officers' allowances are $50.52 a month, or about $1.66 on a daily basis.[1] Over half of all enlisted personnel and all officers receive cash subsistence allowances.

Since neither quarters nor subsistence allowances, whether received in cash or in kind, are taxable, military personnel enjoy a tax advantage. The magnitude of this saving, which is equivalent to the amount of additional cash income that would have to be provided to ensure the same take-home pay if allowances were taxable, in each case depends principally on the size of the allowances, total taxable income, and dependency status. The average benefit now ranges from about $32 to $275 a month.

Taken together, basic pay, allowances, and the tax advantage constitute regular military compensation (RMC). Initially defined by Congress in the Military Pay Act of 1965, RMC is taken to be the military equivalent of the civilian salary. Indeed, between 1967 and 1974 RMC was the basis for linking military and civilian pay and for calculating comparability pay increases. Table 2-1 shows the amounts of RMC for typical service personnel at each military pay grade.

---

1. Enlisted personnel draw larger subsistence allowances than officers do because, before 1974, the rates were set under different procedures. Changes in subsistence allowances for officers had required specific legislation, and a monthly rate of $47.88 had prevailed from 1952 to 1974. Enlisted personnel's allowances, on the other hand, which had been pegged to the cost to the government of procuring food, had traditionally lagged behind officers' allowances until the dramatic increase in food prices that occurred in 1973–74. The formula was changed in 1974, and as matters now stand cash subsistence allowances for both officers and enlisted personnel are increased by the same percentage. Since enlisted personnel were receiving more when this change was made, their subsistence allowances will continue to be higher than those for officers.

Table 2-1. Components of Regular Military Compensation, by Grade, Annual Rates Effective October 1, 1974[a]

Pay grade	Title	Years of service	Number of dependents	Basic pay (dollars)	Quarters[b] allowance (dollars)	Subsistence[b] allowance (dollars)	Average federal tax advantage (dollars)	Regular military compensation[c] (dollars)
Officers								
O-10	General	26	1	36,000[d]	3,647	606	3,291	43,544
O- 9	Lieutenant general	26	2	36,000[d]	3,647	606	3,234	43,487
O- 8	Major general	26	2	36,000[d]	3,647	606	3,234	43,487
O- 7	Brigadier general	26	3	31,565	3,647	606	2,724	38,542
O- 6	Colonel	26	3	27,727	3,272	606	2,137	33,743
O- 5	Lieutenant colonel	20	3	21,856	3,024	606	1,523	27,009
O- 4	Major	14	3	17,640	2,729	606	1,157	22,132
O- 3	Captain	6	3	13,932	2,477	606	905	17,920
O- 2	First lieutenant	2	2	9,580	2,225	606	573	12,984
O- 1	Second lieutenant	less than 2	1	7,610	1,793	606	498	10,507
Enlisted personnel								
E-9	Sergeant major	22	3	13,666	2,333	880	937	17,815
E-8	Master sergeant	20	3	11,380	2,182	880	730	15,171
E-7	Sergeant, first class	18	3	9,907	2,045	880	581	13,412
E-6	Staff sergeant	14	3	8,428	1,901	880	544	11,752
E-5	Sergeant	4	2	6,156	1,757	880	555	9,348
E-4	Corporal	2	1	5,249	1,537	880	522	8,187
E-3	Private, first class	less than 2	0	4,781	914	880	445	7,020
E-2	Private, E-2	less than 2	0	4,601	810	880	412	6,703
E-1	Private, E-1	less than 2	0	4,129	760	880	387	6,156

Source: Based on data provided by the Department of Defense, Office of the Assistant Secretary of Defense for Manpower and Reserve Affairs, October 1974.

a. The example shown for each grade represents a typical person in that grade.

b. Quarters and subsistence amounts are based on cash rates. The values of in-kind allowances differ from cash rates; hence RMC for those not receiving cash allowances would differ from the amounts shown in the last column.

c. Because of rounding, detail may not add to totals.

d. Rates of basic pay for these officers are limited to $36,000 a year by Section 5308, Title 5, U.S. Code. In the absence of this limitation, if annual basic pay for an O-10, an O-9, and an O-8 had been increased at the same rate as that for other officers, it would be $45,630, $40,262, and $36,299, respectively. At these rates, RMC would be about $54,000 for a general, $48,000 for a lieutenant general, and $44,000 for a major general.

Special Pay

Like the private sector, the military offers pay above the average in order to keep certain jobs filled. To meet these specific needs, there are a variety of special payments that augment basic pay. In the main, these special payments are used to attract personnel having particular expertise, to encourage the retention of personnel with special skills, or to compensate for unusual risk or objectionable tasks. Few of these payments would be drawn by one person at any one time; over an entire career, however, most military people qualify for many of them at one time or another. The most important are briefly discussed below.

Bonus Payments

Bonuses of up to $3,000 can be paid to enlist personnel in specialties that the military is unable to fill at standard pay levels. Initially, the bonuses were restricted to combat-type jobs, but the secretary of defense now has the flexibility to pay them to personnel possessing skills or qualifications for which a critical need is perceived. In general, bonus payments have been limited to $2,500 and have been used to attract volunteers who are considered trainable for skills in short supply and who are willing to enlist for longer than normal periods of time.

Enlisted personnel already in the service who possess "critical" skills (those deemed to be in short supply) can be offered bonuses if they agree to reenlist for specified periods of time. These reenlistment bonuses range from about $1,000 to a maximum of $12,000, depending on the severity of the retention problem and the number of years of additional obligated service. Navy personnel qualified in skills necessary to operate nuclear power plants, however, can receive up to $15,000.

Proficiency Pay

Enlisted personnel are eligible for additional monthly payments, called "proficiency pay," designed to attract and retain those with certain skills and to stimulate outstanding performance in any skill. There are two principal categories of proficiency pay. "Shortage specialty pay" is used to complement reenlistment bonuses to sustain adequate manning in critical skills; monthly rates vary from $50 to $150. "Special duty assignment pay" is used to induce personnel to volunteer for selected assignments, for example, recruiting. Personnel on recruiting duty receive up to $150 a month, although special duty pay normally ranges from $30 to $50 a month. Proficiency payments, once widely used, are now being phased out in favor of reenlistment bonuses.

Special and Continuation Pay for Medical Officers

Because health professionals—for example, medical, dental, veterinary, and optometry officers—are difficult to attract and retain in the military services, they are authorized differential payments in three forms: special pay, continuation pay, and bonuses. Physicians, dentists, veterinarians, and optometrists are entitled to special pay, and specific formulas for arriving at the amount are tailored to the degree of difficulty of attracting and retaining the various occupational specialties. Physicians—traditionally the most difficult manning problem—are paid an extra $100 monthly during the first two years of service and $350 a month thereafter. In addition, some physicians are entitled to variable incentive pay (doctor bonus); the amount is based on the number of years they have already served and the length of additional time they agree to serve, but it cannot exceed $13,500 a year. For dental officers, special pay rates are somewhat less; moreover, in place of bonuses dentists are entitled to continuation pay. Dentists in the grades of major through colonel, for example, draw continuation pay equal to four months of their basic pay. Still other, less liberal, formulas apply to veterinarians and optometrists. Other health professionals—for example, nurses, physical therapists, dieticians, and psychologists—receive no special pay.

Incentive Pay for Hazardous Duty

Additional pay is provided to personnel as an incentive to specialize in hazardous duties. The types of incentive pay, monthly rates, and the number of recipients in fiscal year 1975 are shown in table 2-2.

Sea and Foreign Duty Pay

Enlisted personnel are authorized to receive special pay while serving at sea or at certain locations outside the continental United States. This

Table 2-2. Incentive Pay Rates and Number of Recipients, Fiscal Year 1975

Duty	Monthly rates of pay (dollars)	Number of recipients
Flight duty		
Officers	100–245	92,400
Enlisted personnel	50–105	37,900
Carrier flight-deck duty		
Officers	110	300
Enlisted personnel	55	7,600
Submarine duty		
Officers	100–245	2,700
Enlisted personnel	50–105	19,700
Parachute jumping		
Officers	110	3,400
Enlisted personnel	55	25,700
Demolition		
Officers	110	600
Enlisted personnel	55	2,500

Source: Compiled from data in *Department of Defense Appropriations for 1975*, Hearings before a Subcommittee of the House Committee on Appropriations, 93 Cong. 2 sess. (1974), pt. 3.

Note: Data rounded to nearest hundred. Table does not include incentive payments for high- and low-pressure chamber duties, acceleration and deceleration experiments, or thermal stress experiments.

pay, which ranges from $8 to $22.50 a month depending on rank, is intended to compensate for "exceptional rigors of duty caused by climatic conditions, lack of normal community facilities, etc."[2]

Other Pay

In addition, there are miscellaneous pay and allowance categories. "General and flag officer's personal money" is intended to offset unusual personal expenses incurred by high-ranking officers. Rates vary from $500 a year for a three-star officer to $4,000 a year for the chief of each service. "Diving-duty pay," ranging from $65 to $110 a month is paid to persons qualified as divers. Military personnel are also entitled to allowances intended to defray special job-related expenses. These include the initial issue of, or a cash allowance for, uniforms and clothing items and, for enlisted personnel, a monthly payment to maintain their military wardrobe. When assigned to areas outside the United States where the cost of living is deemed excessive, personnel are entitled to

2. *Pay and Allowances of the Uniformed Services . . . and Supplementary Material*, H. Rept. 92-38, 92 Cong. 2 sess. (1972), p. 7513.

payments ranging from 15 cents to $2.45 a day. If military personnel are assigned duties that require separation from their families for more than thirty days, they are entitled to additional pay at the rate of $30 a month.

Fringe Benefits

Supplementing pay and allowances, a variety of nonpecuniary benefits are included in the military compensation package that are of great but perhaps incalculable importance to the personnel and of significant cost to the government. In some cases, the benefits are immediately consumable. In others, the benefits, though deferred and sometimes conditional, represent a current value to the uniformed employee. The major supplementary benefits are outlined below.

Medical Care

Military personnel on active duty are entitled to unlimited health care, including dental and optometry services. Their dependents receive medical care in military facilities, subject to availability.[3] When military facilities are not available, dependents in need of inpatient care are entitled to use civilian facilities under the Civilian Health and Medical Program of the Uniformed Services. Dependents who do not reside with their sponsors may select civilian inpatient care in any event. When civilian care is received by the dependents of active duty personnel, the government pays all expenses except for a charge of $3.70 a day or $25, whichever total is greater. Retirees and their dependents pay a flat 25 percent of the total cost of inpatient care. For outpatient care of dependents in civilian facilities, the sponsor pays the first $50 a year for each dependent, or the first $100 a year for a family with two or more dependents. Beyond that, the government pays 80 percent of the bill for the dependents of active duty personnel and 75 percent for retirees and their dependents. Some types of treatment are excluded, such as well-baby care, dental care, spectacle examinations, and chiropractic care.

3. Dependents, however, are not entitled to normal dental and optometry services. When dependents of members on active duty are hospitalized in military facilities, they are charged at the rate of $3.70 a day. There is no charge for outpatient care.

Commissaries and Exchanges

By shopping at commissaries—military supermarkets—some armed forces personnel realize financial savings. According to the most recent estimates, commissary prices on a nationwide basis, including a surcharge averaging about 4 percent to cover some operating costs, are about 20 percent lower than those prevailing in local commercial grocery stores.[4]

Direct dollar savings gained by shopping at exchanges—military department stores—are not as great. Markups average close to 20 percent, compared with 30 to 50 percent in the private sector. By shopping carefully at large discount stores in the local community, however, military personnel could probably duplicate exchange savings. Unlike commissaries, the exchange system, whose sales totaled about $3.5 billion in fiscal year 1974, is operated on a profit-making basis; the government subsidy amounts to about $50 million, mainly for the transportation of merchandise to overseas locations. Part of the profits is plowed back into improvements and new construction and part is funneled back to military personnel in the form of nonappropriated funds to support welfare activities, such as hobby shops and recreational facilities. In fiscal year 1974, these "dividends" amounted to about $75 million, or roughly 2 percent of total sales.

Retirement Benefits

The military retirement program constitutes the most valuable fringe benefit available to military personnel. When military retirement annuities become vested, after twenty years of active service, retirees are

4. The surcharge covers the cost of operating equipment, supplies, utilities, and merchandise losses and spoilage. Salaries for military and civilian personnel and construction and maintenance funds, which together amounted to about $250 million in fiscal year 1975, are subsidized by the government. Not included are procurement and distribution costs, which for the most part are submerged in the budgets of a variety of military organizations. These costs are not easily identifiable; hence the full cost of commissary operations cannot be precisely defined. Total sales of $2.5 billion in fiscal year 1974 made commissaries the fourth largest grocery chain in the United States, but the future of commissary benefits is clouded. For fiscal year 1976, the administration requested Congress to provide much less money than it has in the past to support commissary operations. It has been reported that the administration plans to make commissaries self-supporting by October 1976. (See *Washington Post*, February 8, 1975.) The prompt reaction

Table 2-3. Annual Retired Pay and Expected Lifetime Retired Pay, Selected Examples for Those Retiring on or after January 1, 1975

Grade and title at retirement		Years of service before retirement	Annual retired pay (dollars)	Expected lifetime retired pay[a] (dollars)
O-6	Colonel	30	22,457	505,106
O-4	Major	20	10,215	310,988
E-9	Sergeant major	30	12,141	310,320
E-7	Sergeant, first class	20	5,421	183,568

Source: Data provided by the Department of Defense, Office of the Assistant Secretary of Defense for Manpower and Reserve Affairs, February 1975.

a. Assuming an entry age of 23 for officers and of 19 for enlisted personnel and no pay or price increases.

entitled to 50 percent of their terminal basic pay. Annuities are increased at the rate of 2.5 percent of basic pay for each year beyond twenty years to a maximum of 75 percent. The system is unfunded and military members make no direct contribution to retirement. Congress makes annual appropriations to meet current benefit payments on a pay-as-you-go basis. The examples of annual retired pay and expected lifetime retired pay for selected military personnel shown in table 2-3 demonstrate the magnitude of these benefits.[5]

In addition, those found physically unfit for further service are granted physical disability retirements. The nature and amount of the benefits depend on the degree of disability. Retired pay under such circumstances, paid to persons with either at least twenty years of service or at least a 30 percent Veterans Administration disability rating, is computed by multiplying the retiree's basic pay by the percentage of his disability or by 2.5 percent per year of active service, whichever is larger, but not to exceed 75 percent of basic pay. If retired pay for the disabled is based on percentage of disability, it is exempt from federal taxes. If based on years of active service, the amount in excess of the retired pay that would be received under the former option is not excluded from taxation.

---

of military personnel and their congressional supporters against this proposal underscores the difficulties involved in making even modest changes in military benefits.

5. The average military retiree now retires in his early forties and receives a pension equal to 55 percent of his final basic pay. During his retirement years, he can expect to receive a total pension that will amount to more than twice the total basic pay received during his active duty years. See Department of Defense, "The Proposed New Military Nondisability Retirement System" (1973; processed), p. 3.

Table 2-4. Effect of Social Security Benefits on Income of Retired Military Personnel, Selected Examples

	Officers		Enlisted personnel	
Item	Colonel	Major	Sergeant major	Sergeant 1st class
Grade at retirement	O-6	O-4	E-9	E-7
Years of service at retirement	30	20	30	20
Monthly retired pay (fiscal year 1975 dollars)[a]	1,871	851	1,012	452
Monthly social security benefits (fiscal year 1975 dollars)[b]	253	216	233	186

Source: Based on data provided by the Department of Defense, Office of the Assistant Secretary of Defense for Manpower and Reserve Affairs, February 1975.

a. Assuming retirement on or after January 1, 1975.

b. Social security benefits are based on the following assumptions:

  1. Benefits are collected at age 65.

  2. The average covered monthly earnings for an O-6 are $390; for an O-4, $302; for an E-9, $341; and for an E-7, $233.

  3. The beneficiary's earnings both before and after active military service are not covered by social security.

  4. The rates shown are for the beneficiary alone; payments would be larger if there were eligible dependents.

Social Security

Since 1956, military personnel have been fully covered under the social security system on a contributory basis.[6] Currently, the service member's contribution, which is matched by the government, is 5.85 percent of the first $14,100 of annual basic pay and is mainly intended to provide continuity of coverage for the large number of service people who do not pursue a military career and who are likely to obtain civilian employment covered by social security. For military personnel attaining retirement eligibility, however, social security benefits stemming from military service supplement military retirement annuities. Table 2-4 shows the magnitude of these benefits for selected retired personnel.

Survivor Benefits

If military personnel die from a service-connected disability while on active duty or following service, their survivors are entitled to dependency and indemnity compensation (DIC) and social security benefits. DIC is provided by the Veterans Administration, based on the person's

6. Though they were not required to contribute, military personnel serving between 1941 and 1956 nevertheless were granted social security credits based on earnings of $160 a month.

pay grade at time of death. At present, monthly payments range from $215 for a private's widow to $540 for a general's widow, with additional amounts based on the number of children. Provisions are also made for orphaned children and dependent parents. In addition, a surviving family, consisting of a widow and dependent children or dependent children only, is eligible for an immediate annuity from social security. A widow without dependent children, however, is ineligible for a full social security annuity until age 62 (or age 60 if willing to accept an actuarially reduced annuity). Eligible beneficiaries of deceased military personnel are also entitled to a lump-sum death gratuity equal to six months' basic pay plus incentive and special pay (including proficiency and "hostile fire" pays) but not less than $800 or more than $3,000.

Leave Benefits

Military personnel, regardless of length of service, accrue annual leave at the rate of two and one-half days a month, or thirty days a year. Unlike the federal civilian leave system, however, the military charges holidays and weekends that fall within a leave period as leave. But military personnel can be provided with weekend passes, which generally allow an extra day off and are used mainly to offset the overtime that service people are required to work without compensation. Finally, there is no limitation on the amount of sick leave that military personnel can take when authorized to do so because of illness or injury.

Separation Pay

Upon retirement or separation, personnel may be entitled to one or more types of separation pay. First, those who have not used all the leave to which they were entitled may receive a lump-sum payment for the unused leave up to a maximum of sixty days.[7] The amounts are based on terminal pay rates and include allowances for subsistence and quarters. In practice, a substantial portion of accrued leave goes unused. For example, the average officer leaving the Air Force in fiscal year

---

7. Technically, ninety days of leave may be accrued; however, except for special rules pertaining to prisoners of war and personnel who are missing in action or on combat-zone assignments, only sixty days may be carried forward to a succeeding fiscal year.

1975 received payment for about forty-five days of unused leave; the average airman collected for approximately thirty-eight days. Also, regular officers separated for nonpromotion, unfitness, or unsatisfactory or substandard performance are entitled to severance pay, the amount depending on the cause for separation and the length of service but in no case exceeding $15,000. There is no similar provision for enlisted personnel. Reserve personnel involuntarily released from active duty after serving a minimum of five consecutive years are entitled to "readjustment pay"; again, the amount depends on the cause for separation and the years of service, but it cannot exceed $15,000. Both severance and readjustment pay are intended to compensate for the financial disadvantage of involuntary removal from military employment.

Unemployment Compensation

Personnel who become unemployed after leaving military service are entitled to unemployment compensation under the laws of the state in which they reside. The federal government, through the Veterans Administration, reimburses the state for all unemployment payments stemming from the claimants' active military service. It is estimated that these payments amounted to about $210 million in fiscal year 1974.

Educational Assistance

By virtue of their active service, military personnel are entitled to a broad range of veterans' benefits. Chief among these is the educational assistance provided by the GI Bill, ranging from college courses to vocational and on-the-job training. Each eligible veteran is entitled to assistance for a period of one and one-half months (or the equivalent in part-time training) for each month of service on active duty. The maximum period of training depends on a variety of factors, but in no case can it exceed forty-eight months. Monthly payments for those in full-time programs are $270 for a single veteran, $321 for a married veteran, $366 for a married veteran with a child, and $22 for each additional dependent. Tuition, books, fees, and other educational expenses are paid for by the beneficiary. Low-interest loans of up to $600 yearly are also made available; repayments are not due until nine months after the borrower ceases to be a student and can be made over a period of

Table 2-5. Components of Military Pay, Allowances, and Benefits and Their Costs, Fiscal Year 1975

Component	Cost (millions of dollars)
Regular military compensation	20,245
Basic pay	15,142
Quarters allowance (cash and in kind)	2,535
Subsistence allowance (cash and in kind)	1,598
Tax advantage (estimated)	970
Special and premium pays	966
Special and continuation pay for medical officers	76
Pay for sea duty and duty at certain places	67
Incentive pay for hazardous duty	291
Reenlistment bonus	322
Enlistment bonus	70
Proficiency pay	126
Other[a]	14
Noncompensation personnel costs	578
Clothing issue and allowance	293
Overseas station allowance	171
Family separation allowance	42
Dislocation allocation	59
Life insurance (extra hazard premium)	6
Burial costs	7
Supplemental benefits	15,580
Retired pay[b]	6,276
Medical care	3,265
Veterans' education[c]	4,042
Social security	845
Unemployment compensation[d]	210
Commissary and exchange[e]	303
Separation pay	496
Death gratuity	11
Dependent's indemnity accrual[f]	128
Mortgage insurance premiums	4
Total	37,369

Sources: Based on data included in the President's budget for fiscal year 1975 provided by the Department of Defense, Office of the Assistant Secretary of Defense for Manpower and Reserve Affairs, March 1974. Costs of medical care obtained from *Department of Defense Appropriations for 1975*, Hearings before a Subcommittee of the Committee on Appropriations, House of Representatives, 93 Cong. 2 sess. (1974), pt. 6, p. 130. Cost of veterans' benefits obtained from *The Budget of the United States Government, Fiscal Year 1976* (1975), p. 144.

a. Includes personal money allowances for flag and general officers, pay for diving duty, and continuation pay for submarine officers.

b. Reflects the estimate of the retired pay appropriation—the amount paid to retirees in fiscal year 1975. On an accrual accounting basis, the costs of the military retirement system for fiscal year 1975, based on actuarial valuation, was estimated to be $3.9 billion, assuming 3.5 percent interest, with no allowance for future pay or price increases.

c. The costs shown for veterans' benefits are estimated expenditures; accrual costs are not available.

d. Budgeted by the Department of Labor. Figures shown are estimated payments to ex-servicemen in fiscal year 1974 and are the latest data available.

e. Excludes military pay, construction (commissaries), and costs of transportation overseas and overseas utilities (exchanges).

f. These are one-year term insurance costs to cover the present value of future benefits to survivors of persons dying or retiring from active duty in one year. The figure excludes combat deaths and disability retirements.

ten years.[8] The future of the GI Bill, however, is uncertain. Pressure apparently is building up to terminate eligibility for people entering the armed services sometime in the future, on the grounds that such benefits should be connected with wartime service only.

Military personnel, while still in the service, are provided tuition assistance to attend classes offered by accredited civilian schools and colleges and to participate in correspondence study. The total cost of these programs has not been disclosed.

Other Benefits

A variety of other benefits made available to military personnel include the following:

—Free legal services.

—"Space-available" travel on military aircraft.

—Federal Housing Administration in-service insured loans, which usually provide military personnel with lower down payments and lower interest rates on long-term mortgages.

The Cost of Military Compensation

The structure of the military compensation system is extremely cumbersome. The major elements of the system—not all of which are accounted for in the defense budget—are summarized in table 2-5 and their estimated costs are shown. It should be noted that this listing probably does not include all the elements that should be considered a part of military pay; by the same token, there is less than unanimous agreement that all the items shown should qualify as items of military pay. Nonetheless, the data in the table provide a rough approximation of the financial costs of military compensation. The large investment in fringe benefits is striking, as is the sheer number of separate compensation elements. When account is taken of the complexities involved in evaluating these elements, it is no surprise that military pay is so universally misunderstood. These misunderstandings give rise to significant, albeit less tangible, costs of their own.

---

8. Title 38, U.S. Code, as amended by P.L. 93-508, December 3, 1974.

CHAPTER THREE

MISPERCEPTIONS
AND THEIR IMPLICATIONS

The misunderstandings that surround the whole question of military pay stem mainly from the complexity of the system. To calculate how much armed forces personnel are paid requires involved appraisals of payments or benefits that may be in kind rather than in cash, conditional rather than certain, and deferred rather than immediate. Each appraisal in itself presents formidable problems; together they make the task almost impossible, with the result that military pay is widely misunderstood by armed forces personnel, prospective volunteers, administration officials, and lawmakers.

The Appraisal Problem

Much of the trouble in appraising the value of military compensation is caused by the large proportion of earnings that are received in kind rather than in cash. In fiscal year 1975, for example, about one-third of total military earnings were received in a form other than direct cash payments. This third consisted mainly of government-furnished meals and accommodations, income tax savings, and an assortment of benefits.

How Much are In-Kind Allowances Worth?

About 50 percent of all military people (1.1 million) live in housing provided by the government, and over 800,000 are entitled to free meals in government dining facilities. In both cases, the cash value to the recipient is hard to measure. In the case of housing, the task is made difficult by the wide range in the quality of accommodations, even among military personnel having the same grade and years of service. Some live under conditions not unlike those in college dormitories. Others, on prolonged maneuvers, may be called upon to live under field conditions. Still others may occupy cramped facilities aboard naval vessels. Moreover, among those provided accommodations of similar quality, regional variations in the cost of private housing and public utilities are bound to influence the value that each person attaches to military quarters.

The cost to the government of furnishing accommodations would provide one estimate of their value. The only figures publicly available (shown in table 3-1), however, have remained unchanged since 1956 and now bear little relationship to the real costs of providing accommodations.[1] In the absence of reliable cost data, the cash allowance paid to military personnel when government housing is not available is the most readily available benchmark against which the value of furnished quarters can be measured. Current cash rates, also shown in table 3-1, vary by grade and marital status. The last major revision of these rates was made in 1971 as part of a program to increase monetary incentives for the all-volunteer military forces. At that time, rates for personnel with dependents were set at 85 percent of Federal Housing Administration (FHA) standards for comparable income groups.[2] Starting in 1974, these allowances were linked to the federal comparability process and are now increased at the same rate as federal civilian pay.

Imputing a dollar value to free meals is also made difficult by wide variations in quality as well as by large differences among military personnel in the quantity of food consumed. The average cost of providing meals would understate their value to those with larger than normal appetites and overstate their worth to those who eat less or who choose to eat elsewhere even though they receive no cash allowance for subsistence. The cash allowances currently provided to those entitled to eat where they choose is likewise inappropriate as a measure of value.

1. These estimates, used as a basis for calculating annual increases in military basic pay under the pay amendment of 1967 introduced by Congressman L. Mendel Rivers, went unchanged apparently to avoid the substantial increases in basic pay that would have resulted. Under the complex Rivers formula, which is discussed later in this chapter and in the appendix, a larger quarters allowance (either in cash or in kind) account would have increased total regular military compensation, which in turn would have called for larger increases in basic pay.

2. This represented a compromise between the House proposal, which would have raised cash allowances for quarters to fully meet the FHA standards and the Senate proposal, which did not include any provision to increase quarters allowances. See *Extension and Revision of the Draft Act and Related Laws,* H. Rept. 92-433, 92 Cong. 1 sess. (1971), pp. 23–24.

Table 3-1. Monthly Cash Quarters Allowances and Estimated Monthly Costs to the Government of Providing Accommodations to Military Personnel
Dollars

	Cash allowances		Estimated costs of furnished accommodations*	
Grade and title	Without dependents	With dependents	Bachelors' quarters	Family quarters
Officers				
O-10 General	243.00	303.90	56.00	400.00
O- 9 Lieutenant general	243.00	303.90	56.00	350.00
O- 8 Major general	243.00	303.90	56.00	300.00
O- 7 Brigadier general	243.00	303.90	56.00	250.00
O- 6 Colonel	223.50	272.70	56.00	230.00
O- 5 Lieutenant colonel	209.10	252.00	56.00	203.00
O- 4 Major	188.70	227.40	56.00	183.00
O- 3 Captain	167.10	206.40	56.00	161.00
O- 2 First lieutenant	146.40	185.40	56.00	150.00
O- 1 Second lieutenant	114.90	149.40	56.00	139.00
Enlisted personnel				
E-9 Sergeant major	138.00	194.40	18.00	138.00
E-8 Master sergeant	128.70	181.80	18.00	138.00
E-7 Sergeant, first class	110.40	170.40	18.00	138.00
E-6 Staff sergeant	101.10	158.40	18.00	136.00
E-5 Sergeant	97.80	146.40	18.00	133.00
E-4 Corporal	86.10	128.10	18.00	126.00
E-3 Private, first class	76.20	110.70	18.00	...
E-2 Private, E-2	67.50	110.70	18.00	...
E-1 Private, E-1	63.30	110.70	18.00	...

Sources: Cash allowances provided by Department of Defense, October 1974. Estimated costs of furnished accommodations are from Department of Defense, "Modernizing Military Pay," vol. 2: "Appendices I through IX to the Report of the First Quadrennial Review of Military Compensation" (1967; processed,) p. 26.

a. Includes annual operating and maintenance costs and initial cost amortized over twenty-five years. For reasons discussed in the text, these estimates, though based on 1956 survey data, have remained unchanged.

Though these allowances are roughly related to the average cost to the government of the rations provided, they do not include the expenses involved in preparing or serving the food, which are estimated to exceed the cost of the food itself. Moreover, those entitled to free meals choose to eat elsewhere at their own expense about one-third of the time.

Tax Advantage

The appraisal problem is further compounded by the fact that quarters and subsistence allowances—whether in cash or in kind—are not subject to federal income tax. The amount of this tax advantage is equivalent to the additional cash that would have to be provided to ensure the same take-home pay if allowances were subject to tax. The calculation of tax savings on cash allowances is far from simple; much depends on the person's tax bracket, the magnitude of the allowances, and dependency status. To illustrate, the tax savings for a typical major (O-4) who (1) receives cash allowances, (2) is married and files a joint return, (3) has no income from outside sources, (4) takes the standard exemption and the deduction that results in a minimum federal income tax, and (5) has no tax credits, amounts to about $1,157 a year— roughly 5 percent of his total regular military compensation (RMC). Computed in this way, annual tax savings range from about $387 for a recruit to about $3,300 for a general officer.[3] Calculating the tax savings on in-kind allowances is all the more complicated, given the tough problems in evaluating the allowances themselves. In either case, the number of military personnel, defense officials, and legislators who understand the concept of tax advantage—much less who are able to approximate its magnitude—is probably very small.

Military Retirement

In appraising military benefits, since retired pay is a reward for service performed, a proportionate part of the eventual retirement benefit should be allocated to each year of active service as it is rendered. This accrued value can legitimately be considered a form of compensation. Expressing this deferred benefit in terms of current military compensation, however, poses difficult problems; everyone does not serve until retirement and, among those who do, the evaluation is influenced by their time preference for income.

Retirement benefits are of value only to those who serve long enough to acquire vested rights. Few do; of every 100 new entrants into the military services in fiscal year 1974, it is estimated that only 12 eventually will qualify for retirement. Thus, any appraisal of the military retirement benefit must take into account the probability of a person serving long enough to receive it.

For those people now serving on active duty who will retire, the an-

3. These figures include federal tax savings only. For those subject to state income tax, the savings would be even greater. Advantages stemming from state tax savings, however, vary widely and are not included in RMC.

Table 3-2. Annual Deposit That Would Be Necessary During Active Service to
Accumulate Commuted Value of Retirement Annuity for Those Retiring
on or after January 1, 1975

Grade	Years of active service	Commuted value of retired pay (dollars)	Annual deposit needed to accumulate commuted value (dollars)
O-6	30	329,469	6,292
O-4	20	181,873	6,329
E-9	30	193,865	3,702
E-7	20	102,694	3,573

Source: Data provided by the Department of Defense, Office of the Assistant Secretary of Defense for
Manpower and Reserve Affairs, February 1975.
Note: A 3.5 percent rate of interest is assumed.

nual value of retirement benefits accrued can be viewed as equivalent to
an amount that, if the military retirement system were funded, would
have to be deposited (at a specified interest) to pay for the benefits resulting from service in that year. For selected examples, table 3-2 illustrates the amount that would have to be deposited annually in order
to yield at retirement an accumulation of funds equal to the "commuted
value" of the expected stream of retired payments.[4] For example, the
commuted value of the annuity of a colonel who retired in January
1975 with thirty years of service—$329,469—could have been accumu-
lated by depositing, in each year of service, $6,292 into a fund earning
3.5 percent interest.

This method of evaluating retirement benefits is appropriate only if it
is assumed that the person will retire. Estimating the value of retirement
benefits to those still on active duty and uncertain of retirement prospects is more involved. First, it depends on whether service will extend
to eligible retirement age and, second, if it does, on grade, years of service, and life expectancy at retirement. All these uncertainties must be
considered in an assessment of the accrued benefit. For this reason, it is
sometimes convenient to express the value of retirement benefits to a
person still on active duty in terms of an average. Overall, the average
value of the accrued benefit—taking the uncertainties into account—is
equivalent to about 22 percent of basic pay.[5]

4. The commuted value of retired pay is the lump-sum amount of money
required at the time of retirement that, if invested at a stated rate of interest,
would be sufficient to provide retired pay throughout the retiree's expected lifetime.

5. This is another way of saying that if the military retirement system was
funded, in fiscal year 1975 deposits equivalent to 22 percent of *everyone's* basic

The limitations inherent in such estimates deserve emphasis. First, they are based on "normal cost" concepts in which static pay levels are assumed; hence they understate the true costs of future benefit payments. The expected lifetime retired pay streams shown in table 3-2 for example, do not allow for future increases in the consumer price index, to which adjustments in retired pay are pegged.

On the other hand, the estimates overstate the perceived value of the benefits to those who are not indifferent to time of receipt. Greater significance is generally attached to benefits received now than to prospective future benefits; the further in the future the benefits are received the less the significance attached to them. This time preference can be represented by the interest rate that a person is willing to pay for consumption now rather than for consumption later and is best approximated by relevant alternatives in the private market. The appropriate rate of interest to use is a most difficult conceptual problem on which economists differ sharply.

Taken together, the imponderables discussed above—the uncertainty of retirement, the difficulties in predicting the grade and years of service at retirement, and the problems in estimating economic behavior and appropriate discount rates—make formidable the task of evaluating retirement benefits. In addition, there are problems in assessing the value of the other perquisites that are carried into retirement by retirees, such as medical care and commissary and exchange privileges.

Health Benefits

The value of health care to people in the military is as difficult to pin down as the value of retirement benefits. Appraisal depends on many factors, including the number of dependents, the state of health of the sponsor and of his dependents, and the availability of services. Those without dependents, on the one hand, would place zero value on the availability of dependent medical care. Similarly, an eighteen- or nineteen-year-old who qualifies for military duty under present physical standards probably has little need for health care. To those with families, however, the value of medical benefits takes on larger proportions.

---

pay—or about 17 percent in terms of RMC—would have to be made to meet the expected future obligations (assuming no pay or price increases) incurred as a result of service in fiscal year 1975.

Table 3-3. Estimated Value of Commissary Privileges as a Percentage of Regular Military Compensation, Representative Examples

Grade and title	Years of service	Number of dependents	Value of commissary privileges as percentage of RMC
Officers			
O-6 Colonel	25	3	0.8
O-5 Lieutenant colonel	19	3	1.2
O-4 Major	14	3	2.4
O-3 Captain	7	3	2.1
O-2 First lieutenant	2	1	0.8
O-1 Second lieutenant	0	0	0.0
Enlisted personnel			
E-9 Sergeant major	23	3	1.2
E-8 Master sergeant	20	3	2.2
E-7 Sergeant, first class	18	3	2.7
E-6 Staff sergeant	14	3	4.2
E-5 Sergeant	5	2	2.3
E-4 Corporal	2	0	0.0
E-3 Private, first class	0	0	0.0
E-2 Private, E-2	0	0	0.0
E-1 Private, E-1	0	0	0.0

Source: Derived from data appearing in *Department of Defense Appropriations for 1972*, Hearings before a Subcommittee of the House Committee on Appropriations, 92 Cong. 1 sess. (1971), pt. 3, pp. 36–37.

The cost to the government to provide health service to the dependents of military personnel is one way to approximate the value of this benefit. According to Department of Defense sources, this cost, on average, amounts to about $250 per dependent per year.[6] Thus the average cost per military family amounts to about $685 a year.

Consumer Savings

Appraising the benefits of accessibility to commissaries is difficult, principally because of uneven consumption patterns. Many variables must be considered, including family size, income class, and availability of facilities. Table 3-3, showing Department of Defense estimates of the relative value of commissary benefits for some representative examples, indicates the extent of the variations involved. As these estimates show, the largest absolute savings accrue to those with the largest

6. Estimate provided by Department of Defense, Office of the Assistant Secretary of Defense for Health and Environment, October 1974.

families. With respect to commissary benefits as a percentage of RMC, those in the middle grades with larger families come out further ahead.

Savings to an individual resulting from exchange privileges, which are modest in comparison with commissary savings, are more evenly distributed since unmarried personnel are heavy users of exchanges. Moreover, the indirect welfare benefits resulting from exchange profits are probably consumed disproportionately among the lower-grade unmarried personnel residing in barracks or bachelor quarters on military installations. Because of insufficient data, however, these benefits cannot be quantified nor can the value that service personnel attribute to them be accurately assessed.

Social Security

The perception of old-age benefits stemming from participation in the social security program is affected by two offsetting factors. On the one hand, since the benefits are not payable until age 65 (or, on a reduced basis, at age 62), they are highly discounted, particularly among young noncareer personnel. According to an interagency committee appointed in 1971 to study the military retirement system, "social security benefits typically are not considered by members as having stemmed from Uniformed Service employment."[7] On the other hand, since a service member's contribution appears on each earning statement and since everyone is eligible for social security benefits whether or not he attains military retirement eligibility, the existence, if not the size, of the benefits is probably more widely recognized than are benefits attached to noncontributory military retirement.

Educational Benefits

Evaluating GI Bill benefits, which are both contingent and deferred, presents particularly difficult problems because of the many options that are available and the uncertainty surrounding the extent to which each might be used. According to the most recent Department of Defense estimates based on data for fiscal year 1973, about 55 percent of personnel leaving the service can be expected to enter a training program

7. "Report to the President on the Study of Uniformed Services Retirement and Survivor Benefits by the Interagency Committee" (1971; processed), vol. 1, pp. 1–5.

within the entitlement period, and those entering training can be expected to remain for an average of 1.75 years. At a cost per trainee year of $2,262, the average cost for each person leaving the service was calculated to be $2,165.[8] This estimate is quite conservative, however, since benefits have been increased substantially since 1973.

Total Military Earnings

It is unlikely that service personnel go through the calculations described above. Whether they overestimate or underestimate the money value of these benefits probably depends on their circumstances and the data available to them. For illustrative purposes, some estimates of total military compensation, based on the preceding analysis, are given in table 3-4. The examples shown are limited; the possible combinations of grade, dependency status, duty assignment, location, and pay entitlements are for all practical purposes boundless. Total compensation is, of course, highly sensitive to the assumptions. The relatively small proportion of total earnings that is received in cash is striking; for example, cash payments constitute about 58 percent of the recruit's pay. The other 42 percent is almost certainly not accurately assessed by the personnel involved—or by legislators. These noncash military earnings go largely unrecognized.

Undervaluing Military Pay

How much do those in the military think they earn? Despite its importance, very little research has been directed toward that question, but the studies that have been done record a systematic underestimation by military personnel of their earnings.

Surveys conducted in the late 1960s among military personnel completing their first enlistment period indicated that they underestimated their RMC by about 24 percent.[9] Since allowances and the tax advantage together account for that same proportion of RMC, many military personnel evidently view their total earnings as principally, if not ex-

8. Department of Defense, Office of the Assistant Secretary of Defense (Comptroller), "Economic Cost of Military and Civilian Personnel in the Department of Defense" (1974; processed), p. 13.

9. Results of a survey by Louis Harris Associates reported in U.S. Department of Defense, "Modernizing Military Pay," vol. 1: "Active Duty Compensation" (1967; processed), p. 37.

clusively, composed of basic pay. This perception, in the view of one analyst, stems from the following: military personnel place a low valuation on in-kind, contingent, and deferred benefits; they consider certain benefits as really being job-related and hence their due; and they "mistakenly believe that housing, subsistence, etc., are fringe benefits and that their total fringe benefits are equivalent to those of the civilian sector."[10]

More startling are the results of an informal poll of the economics faculty at the United States Air Force Academy that disclosed that the "average misestimate of true salaries is probably $2,000 on the downward side."[11] This misperception among those holding advanced degrees in a discipline concerned closely with wages and income underscores the pervasive confusion surrounding the military pay system.

The confusion over military pay is not confined to those in the services; professionals in the pay measurement business also run into problems. A canvass by the Department of Defense indicated that for lending purposes banks and finance companies recognized only 48 percent of RMC received by enlisted personnel in the lower grades.[12] It is equally disturbing—particularly at a time when the services are striving to fill their ranks without conscription—that prospective volunteers are hard put to estimate what their military earnings would be. Youth attitude surveys in May 1974 disclosed that about 20 percent simply didn't know what their starting monthly salary would be. Of those recording an estimate, about one out of five underestimated starting pay by at least 20 percent.[13]

The Implications

As the previous discussion illustrated, assigning a dollar value to many of the elements of military compensation is no mean task. The

10. Steven L. Canby, *Military Manpower Procurement* (Lexington Books, 1972), p. 119. This is an excellent technical discussion of military pay.

11. Eric A. Hanushek and William W. Hogan, "Implications of Paying for What You Get" (manuscript, Department of Economics and Management, United States Air Force Academy, 1973). This sum represents an undervaluation of about 10 percent of total military compensation at the O-3 grade level.

12. Department of Defense, "Modernizing Military Pay," vol. 1, p. 38.

13. Survey conducted by Gilbert Youth Research for the Department of Defense, May 1974. Data provided by the Department of Defense.

Table 3-4. Total Annual Military Compensation under Specified Conditions, Selected Examples by Grade and Rank, January 1975

	Officers			Enlisted personnel		
	O-6 *Colonel*	O-4 *Major*	O-2 *Lieutenant (junior grade)*	E-8 *Senior chief petty officer*	E-5 *Staff sergeant*	E-1 *Private*
Years of service	26	14	2	20	4	0
Number of dependents	3	3	2	3	2	0
Duty assignment	Staff officer	Flight surgeon	Submarine	Flight deck	Munitions specialist	Basic training
Location	Germany	United States	Sea duty	Mediterranean	Thailand	United States
Compensation (dollars)						
Regular military compensation	33,743	22,132	12,984	15,171	9,348	6,156
Basic pay	27,727	17,640	9,580	11,380	6,156	4,129
Quarters allowance	3,272	2,729	2,225	2,182	1,757	760[a]
Subsistence allowance	606	606	606	880	880	880[a]
Tax advantage (average)	2,137	1,157	573	730	555	387
Special and premium pay	...	7,140	1,500	930	192	...
Medical officers	...					
Special pay	...	4,200	...	...	...	...
Bonus	...	(13,500)[b]	...	...	...	...
Sea and foreign duty	...	...	...	270	192	...
Selective reenlistment bonus	...	...	...	...	(2,052)[b]	...
Enlistment bonus	...	...	...	...	...	(625)[b]
Incentive pay	...	2,940[c]	...	...	...	...
Hazardous duty	...	...	1,500	660	...	...

Other pay	2,376	...	180[c]	360	461	990
Clothing allowance	...	...	...	...	101	...
Overseas station allowance	2,376[d]	...	...	...	360	...
Family separation allowance	...	...	180	...	...	...
Benefits	7,312	8,591	1,594	4,786	4,766	990
Retirement[e]	6,292	7,311	...	3,702	4,051	...
Health care[f]	750	750	500	750	500	...
Commissary[g]	270	530	104	334	215	...
G.I. Bill benefits[h]	...	...	990	...	...	990
Total military compensation	43,431	37,863	16,258	21,248	14,767	7,146

Source: Author's estimates.

Note: Because of rounding, detail may not add to totals.

a. Allowances for the recruit are based on cash rates.

b. Figures in parentheses are illustrative bonus payments and are not included in totals.

c. Flight surgeon's assignment calls for regular participation in flying duties, and submarine officer is under way half of the time.

d. Colonel is accompanied by his family and lives in private accommodations in Frankfurt, Germany. Rate shown, effective February 1975, includes a housing allowance of $4.55 a day and a cost of living allowance of $2.05 a day.

e. Retirement benefits calculated as follows:

Present grade	Present years of service	Grade at retirement	Years of service at retirement	Level annual deposit needed to accumulate commuted value
O-6	26	O-6	30	6,292
O-4	14	O-5	20	7,311
O-2	2	does not serve to retirement		...
E-8	20	E-9	30	3,702
E-5	4	E-8	20	4,051
E-1	0	does not serve to retirement		...

f. Health care benefits based on average per capita cost of providing health care to dependents.

g. Commissary benefits calculated as a percentage of RMC, using data presented in tables 1-1 and 3-3.

h. Annual accruals of GI Bill benefits based on assumption that O-2 and E-1 would each undertake educational programs for 1.75 years after serving four years in the armed forces and that others shown would serve until retirement and not use the GI Bill.

sheer number of benefits, the issue of whether certain job-related goods and services provided by the government should even be considered a form of compensation, and the fact that some entitlements are conditional and that some benefits are accrued rather than immediately consumable—all combine to place the measurement of the real value of military compensation outside the reach of almost everyone except a handful of professional pay analysts.

The Department of Defense apparently places little emphasis on conveying to prospective volunteers what their total income would be or in assisting those already in the military to evaluate their true total earnings. This may be due in part to the difficulties in value measurement discussed previously. Of equal significance, perhaps, is the incentive to play down the value of military compensation lest administration officials and legislators take a less benevolent stance with respect to pay and benefit legislation.[14]

Explaining military pay concepts to prospective recruits, all of whom will initially receive quarters and subsistence in kind, generally has been left to recruiters. In the absence of a uniform, orderly approach to evaluating allowances and benefits, the principal focus of necessity has been placed on basic pay. To the potential enlistee, expected military income, expressed as basic pay only, fares poorly in comparison with possible civilian pay opportunities.

Pay and the Quality of All-Volunteer Forces

Compensating military personnel by an amount that is larger than they are aware of could have potentially important implications for the future of the all-volunteer services. Despite the encouraging recruiting experience since the end of conscription, many participants in the decision process, concerned that this successful experience may be closely

14. Before legislation adjusted military pay to a level comparable to that of federal civilian employees, and in the absence of labor-management negotiating machinery, the military had to lobby strongly for its pay increases. Over the years, a standard strategy has developed. The Department of Defense study group directed by Admiral Lester E. Hubbell, described this strategy as follows: "In the process of trying to convince others of how bad pay was so it could get raised—because that was the only way it could get raised in the absence of any accepted standard for what it ought to be—the military sold its own career members on how poorly paid they were. Much of this bad psychology remains as an integral part of the military folklore." (Department of Defense, "Modernizing Military Pay," vol. 1, pp. 57–59.)

related to higher unemployment rates, continue to take a wait-and-see attitude with respect to the ultimate outcome of the volunteer experiment. Until recently, principal attention centered on the "quality" of the armed forces—which is difficult to define, and no adequate yardsticks exist for measuring it. The major cause of this concern had been the declining proportion of volunteers who had completed their high school education and had scored above the 30th percentile on the Armed Forces Qualification Test (AFQT).[15] Among concerned groups, the House Appropriations Committee has been one of the most vocal. As a demonstration of its anxiety, the committee included in the defense appropriation act for fiscal year 1974 a provision requiring that at least 55 percent of total new entrants in fiscal year 1974 be high school graduates and that at least 82 percent score above the 30th percentile on the AFQT.[16] With the exception of the Marine Corps, all services met their quantitative goals under these restraints in fiscal year 1974. And although these legislative limitations were not renewed in fiscal year 1975, all services strive to abide by them.

Nonetheless, some military leaders continue to voice concern over the deterioration in discipline and performance that might accompany the transition to an all-volunteer force. The issue of whether or not this concern is legitimate is beyond the scope of this paper.[17] What is important for present purposes, however is the possibility that judgments of the success or failure of the volunteer concept could ultimately rest

15. Standardized tests are administered to all new personnel. The most commonly used standard is the mental group designation based on the scores of the Armed Forces Qualification Test. This test encompasses word knowledge, arithmetic reasoning, tool knowledge, and pattern analysis. On the basis of test scores, examinees are divided into the following groups representing the range from very high military aptitude (category I) to very low military aptitude (category V):

Mental category	*Percentile score*
I	93–100
II	65–92
III	31–64
IV	10–30
V	9 and below

16. *Report on Department of Defense Appropriation Bill, 1974*, House Committee on Appropriations, 93 Cong. 1 sess. (1973), p. 19.

17. Moreover, it is not clear that the measures now available to measure quality are as directly related to job performance as adherence to them might imply. For further discussion of this matter, see Martin Binkin and John D. Johnston, *All-Volunteer Armed Forces: Progress, Problems, and Prospects,* Report prepared for the Senate Committee on Armed Services, 93 Cong. 1 sess. (1973).

on this issue. It is conceivable that, as the nation returns to full employment levels, recruitment could suffer and greater pressures might develop to "solve" the quality problem by offering additional incentives, by reducing military manpower, or perhaps by returning to conscription. Within limits, however, the quality of the armed forces might be improved by increasing the extent to which military pay is recognized, thus avoiding the possible financial, national security, and social costs associated with the alternatives.

This conclusion is based on the relation between pay and enlistments; that is, the number of people in a given population who would choose to enlist in the military services depends in some measure on the level of military pay. That such a relationship exists is widely accepted; the shape of the curve that represents the relationship, however, has been and continues to be a subject of controversy. At issue is the magnitude of the "elasticity factor" (the percentage increase in volunteers that can be expected for a given percentage increase in pay) and the range over which it may be appropriate (the extent to which results based on empirical data can be extrapolated).[18]

Nevertheless, the interaction of pay perception, elasticity, and the quality of volunteers can be illustrated. In fiscal year 1974, for example, 26 percent of all Army recruits had both completed high school and scored above the 50th percentile on the AFQT. The percentage that could be expected to be in that select group under a range of elasticity factors and of increases in pay perception is shown below:

	Percentage of enlistees who would be high school graduates scoring above 50th percentile if pay were perceived to be:		
Elasticity factor	10% higher	20% higher	30% higher
0.5	27.3	28.6	29.9
1.0	28.6	31.2	33.8
1.25	29.3	32.5	35.8

Thus, if the target population—in this case males between the ages of eighteen and twenty-one who had completed high school and who had

18. The task of measuring pay elasticity has been made difficult by several factors. Obviously, pay is not the only influence on a person's decision to enlist. In addition to general increases in military pay and allowance rates, several other factors simultaneously influenced recruitment during the transition to an all-volunteer force: recruiting and advertising campaigns had been put into high gear; special enlistment bonuses had been offered; enlistees were given a wider choice of

the ability to score above the 50th percentile on the AFQT—had perceived military pay to be 20 percent larger and if the elasticity factor for this group had been 1.0, volunteers from that population would have accounted for 31 percent of total Army recruits in fiscal year 1974, rather than 26 percent. The assumption, of course, is that those volunteers who met the highest standards would have been the first selected by the Army.

In practice, the extent to which this particular group of prospective volunteers would have been influenced by increased pay visibility is hard to predict. On balance, research results, though sparse and inconclusive, do suggest that the quality of the armed forces could be improved by increasing pay perception. To estimate the extent to which it could be improved will require further analysis.[19]

Improvements in quality could obviously be obtained through other means, such as intensified recruiting and advertising, additional financial incentives, or increased options. Additional costs would be associated with each. However, before attempting to "buy" quality in these ways, or reducing combat forces, or returning to conscription, efforts should first be made to get the maximum return from the current investment in military pay.

Setting Military Pay Levels

Also owing in part to the complexities of the pay structure, administration officials and legislators have had difficulty determining the levels at which military pay should be set. This is not surprising—260 separate bills pertaining to 111 pay and allowance subjects were introduced and referred to the House Armed Services Committee during the Ninety-second Congress; on the Senate side, 46 bills covering 30

---

options (for example, choice of job, unit of assignment, or both); U.S. combat forces were disengaged from Vietnam; and unemployment was on the rise. The extent of these influences is yet to be discerned.

19. Estimates of supply elasticity with respect to changes in pay have varied widely. In 1970, the President's Commission on an All-Volunteer Armed Force (known as the Gates Commission) used an overall factor of 1.25 to develop the pay rates considered necessary to attain quantitative goals. More recently, an analysis of calendar year 1973 Army enlistments indicated elasticities ranging between 0.55 and 1.42 for high school graduates and between 0.78 and 1.65 for those who had not completed high school. See D. W. Grissmer and others, "An Evaluation of Army Manpower Accession Programs" (McLean, Va.: General Research Corporation, 1974; processed), p. 53.

subjects were introduced and referred.[20] Pay legislation has understandably been piecemeal and open-ended. Legislators consider each bill separately without fully understanding its relationship to other compensation elements or without being aware of the cumulative costs of all the pay and allowance legislation under review, much less their long-term financial implications.

This weakness in the legislative process has had important consequences for the price of defense manpower, on the one hand, and for further complicating the pay system, on the other hand. The implications are most conspicuously illustrated by the Rivers amendment—legislation introduced by Congressman L. Mendel Rivers that strongly influenced the magnitude and composition of military pay between 1967 and 1974.

This amendment was an attempt to help administration officials and legislators answer the perplexing question of how much to pay the military. Until recently, military pay levels have borne little resemblance to market prices. Conscripted manpower was justified mainly on the basis of patriotism and moral indebtedness to national service, especially during periods of international tension, and was viewed largely as a "free good." Hence, military pay, particularly in the lower grades, was inordinately low. As institutional and social changes occurred in the military establishment following World War II, comparability with the private sector became the criterion upon which most military pay legislation was based.

The comparability concept was not formalized until 1962, when Congress applied it to federal civilian employees to ensure that they would receive rates of pay comparable to those received by private sector civilian employees for the same level of work. It was extended to military personnel in 1967, mainly through the efforts of Congressman Rivers, then chairman of the House Armed Services Committee. Wanting to ensure "that pay of our service personnel will continue its present relationship to that of their classified Federal contemporaries," Rivers sponsored legislation calling for automatic adjustments in military pay to match any increases in civilian pay.[21]

Because of differences in the civilian and military pay systems, a

20. See Senate Armed Services Committee, *Legislative Calendar, Ninety-second Congress 1971–1972* (1973); and House Armed Services Committee, *Legislative Calendar, Ninety-second Congress 1971–1972* (1972).

21. *Congressional Record*, vol. 113, pt. 22, 90 Cong. 1 sess. (1967), pp. 30215–16.

special formula had to be devised for translating civilian pay increases into military pay adjustments. This formula called for increases in RMC to match percentage increases in federal white-collar civilian pay. However—and this is important—instead of increasing each element of RMC (basic pay, quarters allowances, subsistence allowances, and the tax advantage) by the same percentage as that of the civilian increase, the formula applied the military increase to basic pay alone.

How an increase in federal civilian pay was translated into an increase in military basic pay under the Rivers formula can be illustrated with an example. In October 1973, the annual increase of 4.77 percent in federal white-collar civilian pay was matched by an equal percentage increase in RMC. At that time RMC totaled $19,467 million, thus calling for an increase of $929 million (0.0477 times $19,467 million). After allowing for a $22 million increase in the imputed value of the tax advantage, the remainder, $907 million, was applied to basic pay only, thus constituting an increase of 6.16 percent. In this way, an increase of 4.77 percent in federal civilian pay and in military RMC resulted in an increase of 6.16 percent in military basic pay.

This method of calculating military pay increases—viewed as a temporary expedient by its proponents—gave rise to several anomalies that had pronounced effects on the price of military manpower. Packing the entire increases into basic pay (1) disproportionately benefited military personnel in the higher grades, (2) compensated many people twice for the same purpose, and (3) increased to levels higher than they otherwise would be the costs of other elements of military compensation that are denominated in terms of basic pay (for example, reenlistment bonuses, reserve drill pay, retired pay, and separation pay). These anomalies are discussed in detail in the appendix.[22]

It is difficult to estimate what military pay and allowances would be now if that formula had not been enacted by Congress. Perhaps even larger pay increases would have been necessary to attract and retain volunteers in the absence of conscription, or perhaps greater pressures would have developed to increase allowances more than they have been. However, if neither had been the case and if each cash element of RMC since 1967 had been increased at the same rate as federal civilian pay,

22. For a fuller discussion of the Rivers amendment, see Martin Binkin, "Calculating Military Pay Increases: A Reform Proposal," in *Revising the Method of Allocating Future Military Pay Increases,* Hearings before the Senate Armed Services Committee, 93 Cong. 2 sess. (1974), pp. 25–40.

the military payroll in 1974 would have been about $1.7 billion less than it was, a reduction of almost 10 percent.[23]

Partly because of this disturbing trend, Congress passed legislation in 1974 to change the method of calculating pay increases. As matters now stand, each cash component of RMC is increased by the same rate as civilian pay, thus removing a provision that increased military pay more than Congress apparently intended. Left hanging, however, is the issue of how, in the face of the fundamental complexity of the pay system, to reduce the probability that another apparently simple, well-intentioned piece of pay legislation could acquire an institutional life of its own and again snowball into a multibillion dollar burden on the defense budget.

23. This is based on the assumption that increases in basic pay granted in 1971 as a part of the all-volunteer incentive package would have been legislated in any event.

CHAPTER FOUR

UNEQUAL PAY FOR EQUAL WORK:
CAUSES AND CONSEQUENCES

The current complex military pay structure not only leads to misperceptions about the true value of military compensation but also induces inequities and inefficiencies within the system. Although the system may be based on understandable and benevolent policies, its architects undoubtedly did not foresee how it would foster inequities with far-reaching implications as the military establishment underwent substantial change. This change has brought about a situation in which a significant portion of total military pay is based on factors other than work performed; indeed, close to 40 percent of total earnings depends on other things: (1) marital and dependency status, (2) availability of government facilities, and (3) whether a member of the armed forces serves until retirement. As a result, a military career has become more attractive to those with a higher level of needs who, consequently, make greater demands on the defense budget.

The Dependency Factor

The philosophy underlying the military compensation system calls for paying people on the basis of their "needs" rather than exclusively for what they contribute to national security. Hence, military personnel with families are paid more and enjoy greater benefits than those who are single and do the same job. The most measurable differences occur in housing allowances and medical and commissary benefits. The differences are summarized in table 4-1, which lists the annual compensation for two sergeants, both of whom have the same grade (E-5), the same number of years of service, and the same job, but who differ in family

Table 4-1. Comparison of Estimated Compensation for an Unmarried and a Married Sergeant (E-5s) with Four Years of Military Service, Receiving Cash Quarters and Subsistence Allowances

Dollars

Compensation element	Unmarried sergeant	Married sergeant with one child
Regular military compensation	8,778	9,348
Basic pay	6,156	6,156
Quarters allowance	1,174	1,757
Subsistence allowance	880	880
Tax advantage	568	555
Supplemental benefits	...	715
Health care (dependents)	...	500
Commissary	...	215
Total	8,778	10,063

Sources: RMC data provided by Department of Defense. Health care and commissary data derived from analysis in chap. 2.

status. As the table shows, the married sergeant receives about $583 a year more in cash quarters allowances than his single counterpart receives. When adjusted for the tax advantage, the difference narrows to $570 a year. When health care and commissary benefits are included, the difference becomes greater; the advantage for the married sergeant grows to $1,285, or 15 percent, a year. The married sergeant would fare even better if both were provided government accommodations, since the difference in value between bachelor and family quarters is generally greater than the difference between the cash allowances.

The differential would be the more striking if, for example, both men were on sea duty. Although neither would be charged for quarters while on board ship, the married sailor would receive a family separation allowance in addition to a cash quarters allowance. In this case, the monetary advantage would grow to over 30 percent. Though difficult to measure, the impact of this discrimination on the morale, motivation, and hence job performance of unmarried people—who constitute the bulk of first-term military personnel and the target population of potential volunteers—may be great.

It is possible that this incentive structure, by making a military career relatively more attractive to those with families, has contributed to the recent marked growth in the proportion of military personnel who are

Table 4-2. Percentage of Male Military Personnel Who Are Married and Average Number of Dependents per Military Male, Selected Years

Fiscal year	Proportion of military males who are married (percent)	Average number of dependents	
		Per married military male	Per military male
1955	37.8	2.09	0.78
1965	50.3	2.74	1.38
1974	56.4	2.74	1.54

Source: Based on data provided by Department of Defense, Office of the Assistant Secretary of Defense (Comptroller), August 1974. Data for fiscal year 1955 are as of December 1954; for fiscal year 1965, as o September 1964; and for fiscal year 1974, as of September 1973.

married and in the average total number of military dependents. As the data in table 4-2 illustrate, a twofold growth in the ratio of dependents to military personnel over the past two decades was brought on both by a substantial increase in the number of military families and by a modest growth in average family size. The increase in the proportion of new volunteers who are married is particularly noteworthy; only about 7 percent of army recruits were married in 1955, but about 22 percent were married in 1974. Since only 9.5 percent of all males in the target population (ages 18–19) were married as of March 1973,[1] the military seems to be relatively more attractive to those who are married. Adopting a more equitable incentive structure—equal pay for equal work—could contribute to a reversal of this trend.

Budgetary Consequences

Changing the proportions of single and married military personnel would have important financial consequences. If the mix of married and unmarried military manpower in fiscal year 1975 had been the same as that in 1965 and the proportion of each group receiving cash quarters allowances had remained the same, the military payroll would have been approximately $80 million a year smaller. If the mix that prevailed in 1955 had been in effect in 1975, annual savings would have approached $450 million.

A smaller dependent population would also result in substantially lower costs for health services. For example, if the ratio of dependents to military personnel that existed in 1955 prevailed today, dependent

1. U.S. Bureau of the Census, *Current Population Reports,* series P-20, no. 255, "Marital Status and Living Arrangements: March 1973" (November 1973), p. 11.

health care costs would be at least $400 million less than they now are, assuming uniform consumption of health services. At the 1965 ratio, savings would be about $90 million.

The implications of the higher married-to-single ratio are also noticeable in the cost of moving military personnel and their families. In fiscal year 1975, about $1 billion was budgeted to cover dependent travel pay and the shipment of household goods—a figure that would have been about $300 million less if the proportion of married military personnel had been the same as that in 1955. At the 1965 mix, about $100 million would have been saved. Both estimates are based on the assumption that the proportion of family moves would be directly related to the proportion of military families.

All told, if the proportion of families in the current military forces and family size were the same as those of a decade ago, the defense budget would be at least $270 million smaller. A return to 1955 force characteristics could be expected to save over $1 billion a year.

Balance of Payments Effects

The attraction that current compensation policies hold for married personnel also has implications for foreign exchange expenditures. In fiscal year 1974, about 312,000 dependents accompanied about 523,000 military personnel overseas, accounting for foreign expenditures of an estimated $550 million. While the number of dependents overseas is related to factors other than the proportion of military personnel who are married, it is assumed that a reduction in total dependents would be accompanied by a reduction of those deployed overseas. If the proportion of dependents now accompanying their military sponsors overseas were the same as that experienced in 1955, for example, foreign exchange outlays would be about $325 million less than they now are, or roughly 60 percent of the total attributed to military dependents.[2]

National Security Implications

Practices that encourage relatively larger numbers of military dependents also influence U.S. foreign policy and defense strategy. Whether

2. In fiscal year 1955, 269,000 dependents accompanied about 1.1 million military personnel overseas.

or not to establish a home port in Greece for a carrier task group of the Sixth Fleet—an issue debated in 1972—provided a conspicuous example. Although many factors prompted the Navy to press for a home port in Greece, the assistant secretary of defense for international security affairs singled out one in particular:

The decision to seek homeporting arrangements in Greece was based primarily on human considerations. We seek ways to keep families together rather than apart; homeporting in Greece will reduce the long family separations resulting from the current rotational deployments of ships from the United States.[3]

The political implications of the proposal sparked wide debate; some critics of U.S. relations with the reigning Greek military junta questioned whether the benefits that might result from home port negotiations would be worth the political costs. The extent to which different mixes of single and married naval personnel would have changed the outcome can only be speculated upon. The example does demonstrate, however, the kinds of international consequences that can result from having a military establishment geared toward, and a compensation system that encourages, a larger dependent population.

It is also important to consider the effect on the military budget of dependent enclaves in Europe and Korea. In all probability, U.S. contingency plans call for the protection and early evacuation of military dependents if hostilities break out. If military forces were devoted to that purpose, a direct incremental cost could be attached to the presence of dependents overseas. If, on the other hand, forces were diverted that could otherwise be committed to hostilities early on, a military cost would be exacted.

A related case deserves emphasis. The Department of Defense has proposed the deployment of two additional Army brigades to Europe. For purposes of economy, the personnel involved will not be accompanied by their dependents and therefore will only be required to serve a six-month tour of duty abroad. To provide a rotation base for these deployments, however, two additional brigades will be maintained in the United States—a measure that might have been unnecessary if there were fewer military dependents.

3. Testimony of G. Warren Nutter in *Political and Strategic Implications of Homeporting in Greece,* Hearings before the House Committee on Foreign Affairs, 92 Cong. 2 sess. (1972), p. 5.

Availability of Government Facilities

Even among those with the same number of dependents, inequities are present. The location of a person's assignment plays an important role in determining, first, whether he is furnished government accommodations and, second, whether military health care facilities are available for his dependents. Both have an important bearing on his total earnings.

Government versus Private Accommodations

Wide variations exist in the availability of government quarters. On some military installations, particularly the larger operational bases, the bulk of the personnel are provided accommodations. On others, few if any government quarters are available.

Whether or not quarters are available carries important implications. In certain cases, a financial advantage accrues to a person living in government quarters; others gain by receiving a cash allowance. For example, a colonel fortunate enough to be furnished government accommodations, utilities (excluding telephones), maintenance services, and perhaps some items of furniture would probably value them far in excess of the cash amount—currently $272.70 a month—that he would receive if accommodations were not available. On the other hand, the odds are that a seaman who calls a destroyer bunk his home would not place its worth at $76.20 a month—the cash allowance to which he would otherwise be entitled.

On balance, married personnel who are furnished family accommodations on a military installation enjoy a financial advantage over their counterparts occupying private housing. The extent of the advantage, however, can be estimated only roughly. In 1974 a survey of the actual rental housing expenses (rent, maintenance, and all utilities except telephones) being incurred by Air Force personnel living in private accommodations showed that these expenses exceeded cash housing allowances by amounts ranging from about 15 percent for an O-5 to 41 percent for an O-1, or a weighted average of 21 percent.[4]

4. Based on data obtained from the Department of the Air Force, January 1975. This survey was limited to about half of all Air Force installations and may not be representative of the total Air Force population. The most recent compre-

The relative advantages of government versus private accommodations for single personnel are less clear. Those in older barracks, in the field, or aboard ships are obviously at a disadvantage. On the other hand, singles living in private accommodations, while perhaps enjoying a higher standard of quality, are probably having to pay for their comfort.

Military versus Civilian Health Care

Wide variations also exist in the availability of health care for dependents in military facilities. As pointed out earlier, dependents of military personnel are entitled to medical care in military facilities on a "space available" basis. When available, outpatient services are provided free; inpatient care is provided at a charge of $3.70 a day. When military facilities are not available, dependents may use civilian facilities under the Civilian Health and Medical Program of the Uniformed Services. Inpatient care in civilian facilities carries little financial penalty, but those whose dependents use civilian facilities for outpatient care must pay a share of the costs.

In sum, differences in net pay result when cash allowances do not enable military personnel to obtain accommodations of the same quality furnished to others of the same grade and years of service and when military medical facilities are not available. Such differences are inequitable, and like those stemming from differences in dependency status, probably exact a toll with respect to morale, job performance, and retention of personnel.

Inequities in the Retirement System

As mentioned earlier, under the present military retirement system, benefits are of value only to those who serve long enough to acquire vested rights. While the present system does not require an explicit contribution by the individual, it has been held that such contributions

---

hensive survey for which the results were made public was conducted in 1966 and showed that actual housing expenses exceeded allowances by amounts ranging from 5 percent for E-5s to 47 percent for O-6s. See Department of Defense, "Modernizing Military Pay," vol. 1: "Active Duty Compensation" (1967; processed), p. 52.

are implicit since pay rates have been set lower than they otherwise would have been. According to the House Armed Services Committee "military compensation is depressed by 7 percent to reflect an imputed contribution towards the members' retirement."[5] To the extent that this has been true, the net annual earnings for the small minority of military personnel (about 12 percent of the total) who will eventually retire are significantly larger than for those who will not retire.

An example, based on the analysis of retirement benefits in chapter 3, demonstrates the point. The total annual compensation of a sergeant (E-5) in fiscal year 1975 would depend in part on whether the sergeant would remain in service until retirement. Assuming that he would retire, say, at grade E-8 after twenty years of service, the accrued value of the retirement benefit in fiscal year 1975 on a level annual deposit basis would be $4,051. An E-5 who leaves the service short of 20 years, on the other hand, loses all entitlement to retirement benefits and will recover none of the equity that has been ostensibly accumulated as a result of the implicit contributions made during active service. The disparity was summed up by a Department of Defense study group as follows: "[Those] who will not serve to retirement are now being made to contribute part of their own salary to someone else's retirement, in addition to forfeiting any Government contribution to their own retirement equity."[6]

Quite apart from its obvious unfairness, the current military retirement system has also been scored for its inefficiency. Since retirement holds no value to anyone who has not attained twenty years of service, personnel have a strong incentive to remain for twenty years, and defense managers are reluctant to release personnel who have not reached vested eligibility. These factors, coupled with relatively small increases in the value of retired pay beyond twenty years of service, encourage

5. *Amending the Military Selective Service Act of 1967; to Increase Military Pay; to Authorize Military Active Duty Strengths for Fiscal Year 1972; and for Other Purposes,* House Armed Services Committee Report 92-82, 92 Cong. 1 sess. (1971), pp. 24–25. The Senate Armed Services Committee, on the other hand, stated in 1972 that "since there is no accepted comparability system linking the various military and Civil Service pay grades it cannot therefore be reasonably said that military basic pay is being depressed by any percentage as an imputed contribution." (See *Fiscal Year 1973 Authorization for Military Procurement, Research and Development, Construction Authorization for the Safeguard ABM, and Active Duty and Selected Reserve Strengths,* Hearings before the Senate Armed Services Committee, 92 Cong. 2 sess. [1972], pt. 1, pp. 47–48.)

6. Department of Defense, "Modernizing Military Pay," vol. 1, p. 47.

personnel to stay on until they attain eligibility and to retire soon there-after.[7]

With relatively large standing peacetime armed forces, substantial real pay growth between 1968 and 1972, and marked increases in the consumer price index since 1972, these policies have resulted in retired pay costs larger than the framers of the policies could ever have envisioned. In fiscal year 1975, for example, more than 1 million military retirees were collecting a total of over $6 billion. If the present trend continues, by 1980 the number of retirees will have grown to over 1.3 million and the retired pay obligation will have increased to $7.6 billion a year (in 1975 dollars).

7. Recent changes in the national economic picture have served to reinforce the incentive for early retirement. With double-digit inflation, increases in retired pay, which are tied to the consumer price index, have outrun increases in active duty pay. As a result, under present law recent retirees receive smaller annuities than do some who retired previously at the same grade and with the same number of years of service. The administration was expected to advance legislation to the Ninety-fourth Congress to overcome this inversion problem.

CHAPTER FIVE

RECOMMENDATIONS FOR REFORM

The system used today to compensate armed forces personnel—a system geared to meet the needs of the military establishment of an earlier era—is a costly anachronism. Military personnel are apt to understate the real value of their compensation simply because some elements of it come to them in a form other than cash and they do not accurately perceive their value. Further, the system often attracts personnel that are costly in relation to their skills and encourages them to remain in the service.

The implications are far-reaching. As matters now stand, the United States pays more than is necessary to field its military forces; alternatively, for its current level of spending the military could attract higher-quality personnel. Moreover, given the present course, the system promises to become even less efficient as the funds devoted to the principal fringe benefits, retirement and health care, consume an even greater proportion of total military manpower costs.

The recommendations offered here for turning this trend around follow three basic principles: (1) military earnings should be made more visible and understandable, (2) pay differentials based on dependency status or the availability of government accommodations should be eliminated, and (3) the present inequities and perverse incentives of the military retirement system should be removed. The first calls for converting to cash form, wherever appropriate, items of compensation now being received in nonmonetary form. The second calls for the adoption of policies that would pay people for their contribution rather than to meet their needs, and the third could be accomplished by making changes in the military retirement system along lines already proposed within the administration.

Taken together—and it is important that these proposals be viewed as a package—the measures are designed to realign the military pay structure in order to attract and retain the kinds of people needed for national defense at the lowest cost. As the result of minimizing the penalty to be paid by those already in the system, the proposed changes would not yield large savings in the short run; in fact, they might involve an initial increase in costs. Savings would appear within a few years, however, and would become larger over time.

A Military Salary

Many of the problems associated with the lack of visibility could be resolved by paying military people in much the same fashion as federal civilian employees are paid. The present hodgepodge of military pay, allowances, and tax advantage would give way to the payment of a single "salary," which would be subject to normal taxation and from which members of the military would pay the costs of goods and services not directly related to their job, just as civilians do. Earnings would become more apparent, more understandable, and hence easier for everyone to evaluate. Pushing the concept one step further, each person of the same grade and years of service would receive the *same* salary, irrespective of dependency status. The distinction between basic pay and allowances would disappear, and each person would pay for food and accommodations whether obtained from government or private sources.

The concept is not new. At the instigation of Congress, the Department of Defense in the late 1960s undertook a complete structural review of the military compensation system. The conversion to a salary system for career personnel was among the principal recommendations of the Department of Defense study group headed by Rear Admiral Lester E. Hubbell. Though seconded by the President's Commission on an All-Volunteer Armed Force in 1970, the proposal was never advanced to the attention of Congress, in large measure because of the costs—estimated at that time to be about $460 million—to implement the changes and also because of strong opposition among the military rank and file, who have generally opposed any attempts to alter their pay system.

The elements of the present compensation system that should be subsumed under a military salary and the amount at which the salaries should be set are difficult questions in need of further analysis. As a first step, however, military salaries could be equated to existing levels of regular military compensation, calculated at the "with dependents" rates to avoid discrimination based on dependency status. The effect of this proposed arrangement on the net pay of those now in the system would vary depending on their circumstances. To illustrate, the effects are traced for a sergeant (grade E-5) in table 5-1. The results show the following:

First, for married E-5s living on the private economy and now drawing cash allowances, annual salary would exceed current cash pay by $577, the amount of the average tax advantage. This increase, of course, would be illusory; net pay would remain virtually unchanged because the increase would be returned to the Treasury in the form of taxes.[1] The principal benefit of this action would be that members of this group would better appreciate the tax advantage as a significant element of pay.

Second, the salary of married E-5s who occupy government family accommodations would increase by $2,334 over current cash pay. The change in real pay for members of this group, however, would depend on how much they were charged for the government accommodations they occupy. Assuming that the average fair market value of military family housing is about 20 percent higher than the current amount of cash quarters allowances, married E-5s provided government family housing would be charged an average of about $175 a month to cover rent, utilities (except telephone), and maintenance services. Since they now are implicitly paying $146 a month, their annual real pay would be reduced by about $350.

Third, for the relatively small number of single E-5s who live in private accommodations, the additional $1,160 in annual cash pay that they would receive would consist of two components—an increase to equalize the cash quarters rate for those with and without dependents and the monetization of the tax advantage. The former would represent a real increase of $580 in their annual pay.

Finally, salaries for single E-5s occupying government accommodations and subsisting in military dining facilities would be about $3,214, or over 50 percent, larger than their current cash pay. The real increase

---

1. The effect on the real pay of individual members of this group, however, would vary. Since the tax advantage is an average, some would pay more and some less than $577 in additional taxes, depending on outside income, number of exemptions, whether deductions were itemized, and so forth.

Table 5-1. Comparison of Annual Gross Cash Pay and Estimated Change in Real Pay
under Current and Proposed Systems, for Sergeant (E-5) with Four Years of
Service, under Specified Conditions
Dollars

Description	Annual gross current pay[a]	Proposed cash pay	Estimated change	
			Gross pay	Real pay
Married				
Private accommodations	8,793	9,370	577	...
Government accommodations	7,036	9,370	2,334	−350
Single				
Private accommodations	8,210	9,370	1,160	580
Government accommodations	6,156	9,370	3,214	640

Source: Author's estimates based on assumptions discussed in text.
a. For present purposes current gross cash pay is confined to basic pay and cash quarters and subsistence allowances where appropriate. Thus it does not include special or premium payments to which some are entitled. For simplicity, it also does not include the cash payment that might be provided to offset the additional social security deductions that would be required if a salary replaced basic pay.

for these E-5s, as for their married counterparts, would depend on how much they would be charged for government quarters and on the extent to which they formerly had elected to buy their own meals rather than to eat free of charge in government dining facilities. Based on the assumption that the charge for government quarters would be about $117 a month, or 80 percent of the current "with dependents" rate of $146.40 a month and that members of this group, in the absence of a salary system, would continue to eat one-third of their meals on the private economy at their own expense, the real pay for these personnel would be increased by about $640 a year.

As the table illustrates, under this approach most E-5s would be likely to realize that their pay is substantially higher than they perceive it to be. In addition, those who are single would in fact receive real increases in their pay. This is important since this category includes a large proportion of military personnel facing the decision of whether or not to reenlist after an initial term of service. The improved visibility of their pay and the removal of irritating inequities might serve as a greater incentive for single personnel to pursue a military career than does the present system.

The implications of such a change for prospective volunteers would also be important. Under the proposed salary system, a recruit would receive $570 a month, out of which he would pay for food and housing. This would provide a much better basis for comparing military and

Table 5-2. Proposed Military Salaries, Selected Examples, January 1975

Grade and title		Years of service	Annual salary (dollars)[a]
Officers			
O-10	General	26	43,544[b]
O- 9	Lieutenant general	26	43,487[b]
O- 8	Major general	26	43,487[b]
O- 7	Brigadier general	26	38,542[b]
O- 6	Colonel	26	33,638
O- 5	Lieutenant colonel	20	26,922
O- 4	Major	14	22,109
O- 3	Captain	6	17,953
O- 2	First lieutenant	2	13,041
O- 1	Second lieutenant	less than 2	10,583
Enlisted personnel			
E-9	Sergeant major	22	17,770
E-8	Master sergeant	20	15,119
E-7	Sergeant, first class	18	13,406
E-6	Staff sergeant	14	11,768
E-5	Sergeant	4	9,370
E-4	Corporal	2	8,220
E-3	Private, first class	less than 2	7,499
E-2	Private, E-2	less than 2	7,320
E-1	Private, E-1	less than 2	6,838

Source: Author's estimates derived from Department of Defense RMC data based on basic pay rates that were in effect in September 1974 and the assumption that all personnel would be paid cash quarters allowances at the "with dependents" rate. These data were revised upward by 5.52 percent to account for the pay raise in October 1974. Since the average tax advantage did not increase by exactly 5.52 percent as did the other elements of RMC, the estimates should be viewed as approximations.

a. For simplicity, does not include the cash payment that might be provided to offset the additional social security deductions that would be required if a salary replaced basic pay.

b. Salaries shown for general officers are based on basic pay rates that are now limited to $36,000 a year by Section 5308, Title 5, U.S. Code. If the $36,000 ceiling were applied to the proposed military salaries as it now is to civilian salaries, general officers would lose the amount of their present allowances and tax advantage—over $7,000 a year. On the other hand, were the ceiling removed and retroactive increases allowed, salaries would be as follows: $53,866 for an O-10; $47,993 for an O-9; and $43,594 for an O-8.

civilian job opportunities than does the current system under which a recruit receives $344 plus food and accommodations. Moreover, a recruit's take-home pay would be larger than it now is since any charges for housing would be unlikely to match the increased cash income included in his salary for this purpose.

Table 5-2 gives examples of the salaries that would be paid under this proposal to typical military personnel in each grade. The improved visibility and equity stemming from these changes would have budgetary implications. A larger cash payroll would result since those now provided government accommodations and food (and not receiving cash allowances) would receive the same salary as those now receiving cash payments. This would add about $2.6 billion to the cash payroll. Of this increase, about $1.8 billion would be included in the salaries of those living in government housing or of single personnel who now receive cash quarters allowances at the lower "without dependents" rate. The remaining $800 million would be included in the salary of those— principally lower-grade single personnel—who do not now receive cash subsistence allowances.

A large portion of these additional expenditures, however, would be recovered through collections for meals and housing provided by the government. The amount that would be recouped would depend on a variety of factors and can only be roughly estimated. Of the $800 million that would be distributed to those now entitled to free meals in government facilities, a minimum of $530 million should be recoverable either through charges for meals furnished in government dining halls or for the smaller government food purchases that would result if more personnel, upon receiving cash allowances, chose not to eat in government dining halls. The remaining $270 million, which would be received by those who do not now receive cash food allowances but nevertheless choose not to eat all meals in military facilities, would not be recovered.[2] If, as a result of these changes, fewer personnel chose to eat in government facilities, additional savings would be bound to occur since fewer support personnel (cooks, servers, etc.) would be needed, and perhaps some dining halls could be consolidated and others closed.

Estimating the portion of the $1.8 billion that would be recovered through rental charges for government accommodations is more difficult. Variations in the quality of housing, regional market differences, and in some cases the lack of individual choice make it difficult to devise rental rates that would appear fair to everyone. The Hubbell study group proposed that collections for government quarters be set "at the lower of: (1) fair rental value of quarters furnished or (2) the 75th percentile of housing expense for FHA mortgagees of equal salary."[3] Under that

2. This cost, however, would be almost offset by the savings that would accrue if the markup in commissaries were increased to cover their full operating costs, as recommended by the administration. There is a logical basis for this offset; it would reallocate to single personnel benefits in subsistence now enjoyed disproportionately by married personnel.

3. The second constraint was apparently intended to protect senior personnel from paying unusually large rents on quarters that they might occupy. The fair market rental value of general officer quarters at Fort McNair in Washington, D.C., for example, would far exceed the cash housing allowance of $304 a month.

criterion, the group estimated that about three-fourths of the cash allowances paid to those living in government accommodations would have been retrieved.

More recently, the Department of Defense has estimated that if married personnel occupying government accommodations were charged at a rate equal to their cash allowances and single personnel were charged at half the current single cash rate, all but about $465 million would be recovered. If no collections were made from single enlisted personnel, all but $800 million would be retrieved.[4]

In this calculation, however, no account was taken of the possibility of collecting larger rental fees from personnel who are occupying government accommodations that are worth more on a fair market basis than their cash allowances. The extent of this offset, though difficult to estimate, could be sizable. To illustrate, if it is assumed that the average quality of family housing furnished by the government is on a par with the accommodations being procured by military personnel living on the private economy, the average fair market value of government-furnished housing would be equal to the average amount being paid for private accommodations. Since the Air Force survey results discussed earlier suggest that military personnel are paying about 20 percent more for private rental housing than the cash allowances they now receive,[5] it reasonably follows that fair market rental rates for government-furnished quarters could legitimately exceed the amount of the current cash allowances. If rental charges for those occupying family quarters were set, say, an average of 20 percent higher than their cash allowances, the full $1.8 billion would be recovered, even if those occupying bachelor facilities were charged, on average, only 80 percent of the additional cash they would receive. Less liberal policies with respect to single personnel, of course, would result in a net savings. In any event, an appropriate and equitable rate structure that would at least retrieve the full increase is a

---

On the other hand, the Hubbell proposal would have provided field or ship accommodations free of charge. See Department of Defense, "Modernizing Military Pay," vol. 1: "Active Duty Compensation" (1967; processed), p. 55.

4. *Revising the Method of Allocating Future Military Pay Increases,* Hearings before the Senate Armed Services Committee, 93 Cong. 2 sess. (1974), p. 21. Adjusted to include the effects of the pay increase of October 1974. Under the first option—charging single enlisted personnel at half the current single rate—recruits would pay rent at a rate of $31.65 a month; second lieutenants living in bachelor quarters would pay $57.45 monthly.

5. Data provided by the Department of the Air Force, January 1975.

reasonable prospect. This approach would not only serve to increase the net benefits of single personnel in the lower grades, but would also remove the inequities stemming from whether or not a person is furnished government accommodations.[6]

As discussed above, the salary paid to each person under this approach would also include in cash form the tax advantage that is now implicit in RMC. This would increase the military payroll, and hence the defense budget, by an estimated $1.2 billion. Since this amount would be returned to the Treasury in the form of taxes, however, federal spending would not be affected. Transferring the tax advantage—a real cost to the taxpayer—to the defense budget would be appropriate inasmuch as the cost would then be charged to the program responsible for it instead of being buried as it now is in reduced federal revenues.

Finally, if a salary replaced basic pay, those who are now making social security contributions of less than the maximum (most enlisted personnel but few officers) would be faced with increased deductions, which would be matched by the government. According to Department of Defense estimates, this would cause an increase of about $640 million in the defense budget.[7] Although federal spending would be unaffected in the short run since social security is on a pay-as-you-go basis, additional costs would be absorbed by taxpayers in the future when the increased benefits were paid.

Special formulas would have to be developed to deal with those elements of compensation that are now pegged to basic pay rates; for example, reserve drill pay, separation pay, and reenlistment bonuses. These payments should not be increased simply as a result of adopting a salary system. Indeed, the improved visibility of pay that would accompany the conversion to a salary system should reduce the need for, or

6. This is not to suggest, however, that the establishment of such a rate structure would be easy. Because of wide regional variations, responsibilities would have to be delegated to local installation commanders. Over time, the implications of establishing fair market rental rates could be significant. A better basis would be provided for assessing the cost effectiveness of maintaining present quarters and of constructing new facilities.

7. To ensure no reduction in the current real pay of military personnel as a result of increasing social security coverage, it is assumed that the pay of those affected would be increased by the amount of the additional social security contribution they would be required to make. It could be argued, on the other hand, that the cost of the increased benefits should be absorbed by the employee. In that case, the defense budget would be increased by only $320 million—the amount of the government's matching contribution.

Table 5-3. Summary of Average Annual Costs to Convert to a Military Salary System
Millions of fiscal year 1975 dollars

| | Spending implications | |
| | Department | |
Calculation	of Defense	Federal
Provide all personnel:		
Cash food allowances	800	800
Cash housing allowances at current "with dependents" rate	1,800	1,800
Monetize tax advantage	1,250	...
Increase social security contributions	640	...ᵃ
Total budget increase	4,490	2,600
Less offsets:		
Subsistence collections or reduced food costs	530	530
Quarters collections	1,800	1,800
Commissary price markup	250	250
Total offsets	2,580	2,580
Net direct costs	1,910	20

Source: Author's estimates based on discussion in text.
a. Increased federal spending would occur gradually as those now in the system became eligible to receive the increased benefits, and would not reach measurable proportions for at least 20 years.

the amount of, reenlistment bonuses rather than increase the base to which these bonuses are tied.

In sum, the calculations above suggest that the conversion to a salary system along the lines specified would result in an average annual increase in *defense spending* of about $1.9 billion in fiscal year 1975 dollars, but in only a small increase in total *federal spending*, as table 5-3 shows. Over time, savings would be expected to grow as the need for differential payments was reduced, as changes in the dependent-to-military ratio took place, and as more appropriate pay increase formulas were developed. Moreover, the corollary to this measure—a realignment of the fringe benefit structure—could lead to substantial savings over the long term. These possibilities are discussed below.

Changes in Fringe Benefits

Current military retirement and health care programs, the principal fringe benefits for armed forces personnel, are products of an era characterized by inordinately low pay for most military personnel. At one time, there was good reason to provide generous fringe benefits as a partial offset to low pay. Events of the past decade, however, have brought such traditional views under question. Substantial increases in military basic pay have been granted, both in the interest of equity and to provide the incentives considered necessary to meet the goals of the all-volunteer experiment, and the end of conscription also called for rather substantial improvements in the standard of living for armed forces personnel. By most accounts, military pay has reached rough comparability with federal civilian pay. Moreover, recruiting experience since the end of conscription indicates that military pay is sufficiently competitive to attract and retain the number, if not the quality, of volunteers required for the armed forces. By almost any standard, whether the scale of pay or the special characteristics of military life, the expensive benefit structure is now more difficult to justify. And with the greater appreciation for true earnings that the salary system proposed above would bring to the military, the need to assess current benefits becomes all the more pressing.

Military Retirement Reform

As a result of the disturbing trend in the annual costs of military retired pay—projected to reach over $13 billion (in 1975 dollars) by the year 2000—the President appointed an interagency committee in 1971 to study the military retirement system and to develop legislative proposals for changing it. That committee, composed of representatives of the Department of Defense, the Office of Management and Budget, the Veterans Administration, and the Civil Service Commission, concluded that the current nondisability retirement system was inefficient, inequitable, and costly.[8] Essentially, the committee proposed that military retirement should be aligned with the federal civilian retirement system. The broad features of these proposals were as follows:

—To increase benefits for those remaining in the service more than twenty-five years and to reduce benefits for those staying less. This change would have the effect of reducing personnel turnover in the active service as well as the total cost of retired pay.

—To eliminate inequities, retired pay would be based on the average of the highest three consecutive years, as in the federal civil service, rather than on terminal pay.

8. "Report to the President on the Study of Uniformed Services Retirement and Survivor Benefits by the Interagency Committee" (1971; processed), vol. 1, pp. 1–3.

—To reduce social security benefits for military retirees. The offset from the service annuity would be one-half of the social security retirement benefit attributable to military service.

—To establish vesting provisions for personnel who leave the services before serving twenty years. For those separating voluntarily with between ten and twenty years of service, equity payments (lump-sum or deferred annuities) would be made; for those separating involuntarily after five years of service, readjustment pay would be provided.

—To align military survivorship benefits with those applicable to federal civil service retirees.

—To make comparable changes in retired benefits for reserve personnel.

The vesting provisions advocated in this proposal represented a step toward removing existing inequities and providing greater management flexibility. However, the committee stopped short of recommending that military personnel contribute explicitly toward their retirement as do federal civilians. Accommodating that provision would not be difficult. Gross pay for each person could be increased by the amount of the contribution and an offsetting deduction could be shown on the pay statement. This would provide armed forces personnel with a greater appreciation for retirement benefits as they were being accrued. The size of the contribution would depend on the benefit provisions that were adopted.

The committee also addressed itself to the problem of whether military retired pay increases, which, like increases for federal civilian retirees, are now pegged to changes in the cost-of-living index, should be recomputed each time there is a real increase in active duty pay. Recomputation was the rule before 1958, and there is considerable pressure from military retirees to resume this practice. The committee recognized that there were some arguments for doing so but, given the offsetting considerations, concluded that a return to continuing recomputation was unwarranted. As a compromise, it recommended a one-time recomputation for persons now retired, which would be made under specified conditions as to age and length of service.[9]

9. Efforts to adopt recomputation were rejected by Congress in 1972, 1973, and 1974. In 1974, the administration withdrew the active support of the proposal that it had advanced in the previous two years. Inasmuch as no other government retirement plan includes provisions for recomputation, it should not be considered as a necessary part of retirement reform.

These proposals, generally based on the principle that those already in the system should not be penalized, also included save-pay provisions that would guarantee retirees at least as much retired pay as that collected by those of the same rank and years of service who retired earlier. Hence reforms undertaken under this premise would save little initially but would begin to have a significant and growing cost-saving impact after several years. For example, first-year costs of about $200 million (to accommodate retrospective lump-sum payments, increased multipliers for longer service, and save-pay provisions) would give way to estimated annual savings of about $400 million by 1985 and of more than $4 billion by the end of the century. Average annual savings over the period would amount to over $1 billion.[10]

The proposals of the interagency committee were reviewed and modified within the Department of Defense. The amended package, significantly more liberal than the federal civilian retirement system and generally not going as far as the recommendations of the interagency committee, was submitted to Congress in 1973. The proposal, however, was not given a warm reception. A subcommittee of the House Armed Services Committee held hearings for three days during the 1974 lame-duck session, but the Senate Armed Services Committee never took up the bill.

Such proposals often founder because they are complex, they appear to penalize those in the military services, and they emphasize long-term rather than immediate savings. Military retirement, however, is a key issue that has to be faced. The stakes are high; the financial consequences are potentially greater than those involved in the major debates over force levels and weapon systems.

Dependent Health Care

As indicated earlier, the cost of the military health care system in fiscal year 1975 exceeded $3.2 billion, up 28 percent since fiscal year 1972. Inflationary effects aside, this growth has stemmed mainly from the increased use of medical facilities by a fairly constant number of total eligible beneficiaries. Even if the number of active duty personnel remains fairly constant, the cost of the program will continue to rise,

10. Too much precision should not be attached to these estimates, however, since they are highly sensitive to assumptions about future pay and price patterns. The estimates shown are based on future increases of 5 percent a year in military basic pay and 1.5 percent a year in the consumer price index.

since the total number of beneficiaries is expected to grow as the retiree and dependent population increases. In fiscal year 1975, of about 9.6 million total eligible beneficiaries, active military personnel constituted about 2.2 million, or only 23 percent.

The administration, concerned about this trend, initiated a study of the military health care system in 1974. A team composed of representatives of the Office of Management and Budget, and the Departments of Defense and of Health, Education, and Welfare was formed to assess the ability of the current military medical program to meet the future needs of the armed forces. This group, whose findings were expected to become available in mid-1975, was charged with evaluating the existing system and alternatives.

The issues are much too complicated to address in detail in this short paper. Nonetheless, some broad options for making the system more efficient and equitable can be outlined.

First, the establishment of a program that would levy a charge for outpatient care of dependents in military facilities would help to remove the advantage that those able to use military facilities currently enjoy over those who use the cost-sharing Civilian Health and Medical Program of the Uniformed Services (CHAMPUS). A rate schedule that would charge, on average, about $10 for each dependent outpatient visit would approximately equalize the cost to the individual for either option and would reduce the current cost of the health care program by about $250 million a year, assuming a constant dependent outpatient load.[11]

Under another approach, the current system could be more closely aligned with federal civilian programs. Military personnel with dependents could by choice enroll them in a Blue Cross–Blue Shield–type of program. As in the case of federal civilians, the cost could be shared; for federal employees the government now pays 60 percent of the cost of the premiums.

Considerable savings would be involved. Were dependents of active

---

11. Dependents of active duty personnel who use military medical facilities visit them an average of six times a year. Were those same visits made to a civilian health facility under the CHAMPUS program, the average cost per visit to the patient would be about $10. This estimate is based on the fact that, under CHAMPUS, the patient would pay the first $50 and 20 percent of the remaining costs in a year and on the assumption that the average cost of a visit (including laboratory fees and drugs) would be about $20. Thus, the patient would pay fully for the first 2.5 visits and 20 percent of the remaining 3.5 visits, or a total of $64 for the six visits.

duty military personnel placed under such a program, the average annual cost per family to the government would be reduced from about $660, the estimated cost of providing care in military facilities, to about $290, for a total annual saving that could reach $450 million, assuming, of course, that the military sponsor would pay 40 percent of the costs of dependent coverage.[12] Even if the government paid the full cost, savings would still approach $225 million a year. Further savings would also stem from enrolling an estimated 2.4 million dependents of retirees in such a program. These savings, however, are difficult to estimate because the per capita cost of providing such care under current programs is not known. Assuming that this cost does not vary significantly from that pertaining to the dependents of active duty personnel, the savings estimated above could well be doubled.

The latter approach, however, would most likely be criticized on the premise that military medical capacity is based on contingency and mobilization requirements and that dependent care presents an efficient way to use slack capacity in peacetime. Moreover, dependent care has also been defended as necessary to foster medical professionalism.[13]

Mobilization requirements, however, are far from clear. In fact, the validation of these requirements is being undertaken by the Department of Defense. It is likely that current policies with respect to dependent care sustain requirements that are in excess of contingency needs. Moreover, even if analysis of mobilization needs supports the current size of the military health complex, opening these facilities in the continental United States to the public when space is available would be an alternative means of achieving the objective and therefore merits further consideration. Under these conditions, military medical centers could establish rate structures that would be competitive with civilian facilities.

12. Based on an estimated monthly cost for family coverage alone of about $44.

13. The legal requirement to provide medical care in military facilities extends only to uniformed personnel. As a matter of policy, however, the services feel obligated to provide medical care to nonuniformed personnel. In 1972, Assistant Secretary of Defense Richard Wilbur gave the following reasons: (1) it would be professionally unattractive for career physicians to see only relatively healthy young males; (2) in order to obtain recognition of military residency training programs from civilian accrediting bodies, a proper mix of patients is necessary; and (3) there is a moral obligation to retired personnel stemming from the implied guarantees for military medical care. (Statement of Richard S. Wilbur, in *Subcommittee No. 2 Hearings on H.R. 16608 . . . and H.R. 14545. . . .* House Armed Services Committee 92-70, 92 Cong. 2 sess [1972], pp. 16285–86.)

The largely unanswered question of how the adoption of a national health care program would affect the military establishment adds to the complexity of the issue. In England, for example, both military personnel and their dependents participate in national health programs, and military facilities are open to the public on a space-available basis.

The best course can be prescribed only after detailed analyses are completed. It is safe to conclude, however, that improvements in equity and efficiency are necessary and that the stakes are high. As in the case of the military retirement system, it is important that changes be made in the health care system in the context of its place in the overall military compensation system.

In Conclusion

This analysis has been directed principally toward identifying various means of streamlining the military pay system so that the best use can be made of the money spent on the military payroll. The measures proposed—paying salaries to military personnel, modernizing the military retirement system, and revising the dependent health care system—would align the incentive structure to the needs of today's armed forces by:

—Providing military personnel and prospective volunteers with a better understanding of military earnings and hence providing a more accurate basis for comparing military and civilian pay opportunities.

—Providing executive branch officials and Congress with a better basis than they now have for assessing how much military pay should be.

—Removing many of the inequities in the current system that appear to be attracting and retaining an increasing proportion of those with dependents.

Taking steps to help military personnel and potential recruits to perceive the value of military pay more realistically could be expected to reduce the need for the number and amount of differential payments (bonuses, proficiency payments, etc.) now used to attract and retain volunteers. Moreover, it is likely that improved perception of pay would result in volunteers of higher quality, as measured by standardized military tests and level of education. Improving the understanding of military pay among administration officials and lawmakers would make it less likely that future increases in pay might be larger than necessary.

Removing discrimination in the present system could slow, and perhaps reverse, the trend toward a higher ratio of dependents to military personnel that has been partly responsible for the growing price of defense manpower. This could be done mainly by increasing the real pay of single personnel at the expense of those who are married, especially of those occupying government-furnished family accommodations.

It is impossible to predict the financial implications of these actions with precision. Based on the analysis in this paper, however, it is estimated that even under the most conservative assumption for each measure proposed, the annual cost of military manpower would be reduced by at least $1 billion and perhaps by as much as $2 billion within fifteen years. These savings could serve to reduce defense spending or to buy a more effective military force for the same money.

These proposals as a whole move strongly in the direction of monetizing military pay and bringing some coherence to an anachronistic, cumbersome, and inherently wasteful system of compensation. They are designed to replace a paternalistic system, justified during a period when military pay was discouragingly low, with a market system comparable to that which exists in the rest of our society—an action made practicable by present military pay scales.

This is not to imply that reform will be easy; difficult questions are involved that will require accepting disadvantages in some instances in order to achieve a substantial improvement in the defense program as a whole. Reform measures therefore require careful study and experimentation.

Traditionally, proposals to reform the pay system have made little headway, principally because of the complexity of the compensation system itself, the misunderstandings that surround these proposals, and the absence of dramatic, immediate savings. But the problem will not go away. If reform is not undertaken, the cost of military manpower will continue to impose a growing and inevitably insupportable burden on the defense budget, with serious adverse consequences for programs to meet more pressing national security and domestic needs.

The Anomalies of the Rivers Amendment

Between 1967 and 1974, annual military comparability pay increases were adjusted by a formula that put the equivalent of the total federal civilian increase into only one element of military compensation—basic pay. This practice, stemming from an amendment introduced in 1967 by Congressman L. Mendel Rivers (1) disproportionately benefited military personnel in the higher grades, (2) compensated many people twice for the same purposes, and (3) increased to levels higher than they otherwise would have been the costs of other elements of military compensation denominated in terms of basic pay (for example, reenlistment bonuses, reserve drill pay, and retired pay). Each is discussed below.

Disproportionate Increases for the Upper Grades

Granting across-the-board increases in basic pay, as the Rivers formulation called for, resulted in larger overall pay increases for personnel in the higher grades. This occurred because basic pay constitutes a larger proportion of total regular military compensation (RMC) for the higher grades (82 percent for a colonel, compared with 64 percent for a corporal). Moreover, because of the progressive nature of income tax schedules, the rate of increase of the tax advantage on a fixed amount of allowances is larger in the higher income brackets. This means that for the same percentage increase in basic pay, the percentage increase in taxes on a fixed amount of allowances is greater for those in the higher grades. Since those allowances are nontaxable, the tax advantage —and hence RMC—increases at a greater rate at higher income levels

Table A-1. Comparison of the Effect of the 4.77 Percent Increase on Average
Regular Military Compensation, by Grade, October 1973

	Officers			Enlisted personnel	
Grade		Percentage increase in RMC	Grade		Percentage increase in RMC
O-6		5.42	E-9		5.18
O-5		5.27	E-8		5.02
O-4		5.13	E-7		4.71
O-3		5.18	E-6		4.48
O-2		5.01	E-5		4.50
O-1		4.63	E-4		4.65
			E-3		4.64
			E-2		4.89
			E-1		4.78

Source: Based on data provided by the Department of Defense, Office of Assistant Secretary of Defense for Manpower and Reserve Affairs, January 1974.

than it does at lower income levels. The combined effects are illustrated in table A-1, which compares the increases in RMC for each grade level that resulted from the increase in military basic pay in October 1973. As can be seen, most officers received increases in RMC that were above the average, offsetting the large proportion of enlisted personnel whose RMC was below the average. Thus, while average RMC increases were on a par with the civilian increases to which they were linked, the distribution around that average worked continuously to widen the differences in pay between the higher and lower grades.

Duplicate Compensation

The Rivers formula also worked to compensate many military personnel twice for the same purpose. Those who received allowances in kind benefited twice, as did those who received cash allowances, though in different ways.

More than half of all military people live in housing provided by the government (barracks, bachelor quarters, or family housing), and close to half of all enlisted personnel are entitled to meals in government dining facilities. Those who receive these services in kind are not entitled to cash allowances. Nevertheless under the Rivers formula, they were being compensated in cash, through increases in their basic pay, to offset the inflationary growth in the cost of housing and meals, and, at the same time, the Department of Defense was paying the increased costs of providing these services. For example, in fiscal year 1974, the cost of operating and maintaining military family housing increased, on an average, from $1,443 a unit to $1,654 a unit, resulting in an increase in defense expenditures of about $90 million. During the same period, those occupying government quarters received, as part of their basic pay, cash payments amounting to $35 million to offset the growth in the cost of housing.[1] Similarly, in fiscal year 1974 the cost of providing meals in government dining halls increased by an average of about $230 a person on an annual basis. In addition to bearing this increased cost —which totaled about $225 million—the government also provided to those receiving these meals, as a part of their basic pay increase, cash payments totaling $24 million to offset the increase in the price of food.

The formula also worked to provide double increases to some who receive cash allowances for quarters and subsistence. The most conspicuous duplication occurred for the more than 1 million enlisted personnel who received cash subsistence allowances. This is because, in addition to annual comparability increases, part of which were designed to offset increases in the price of food in the private sector, other legislation provided for independent adjustments in cash subsistence allowances based on changes in the cost of food to the government.[2] During the period 1967–74, seven adjustments were made in cash subsistence allowances for enlisted personnel, as table A-2 shows.

More than 1 million military personnel who did not occupy government housing also benefited inasmuch as their cash allowances, left unchanged by the comparability formula, appeared to be too low. For example, Congress increased allowances for quarters in fiscal year 1972 as a part of the volunteer-service incentive package. Although both the administration and the Senate proposed to confine the large pay increases to basic pay and bonuses, and notwithstanding the 26 percent increase in quarters allowances that had been reflected in basic pay by that time, the House bill provided "substantial increases in quarters al-

1. For fiscal year 1974, $628.6 million was budgeted for operations and maintenance of 380,006 family housing units, compared with $537.5 million for 372,421 units in fiscal year 1973. See *The Budget of the United States Government— Appendix, Fiscal Year 1973* (1972), p. 327; and *The Budget of the United States Government—Appendix, Fiscal Year 1974* (1973), p. 318.

2. Section 402, Title 37, U.S. Code, specified that the "allowance for enlisted members . . . shall be equal to the cost of the ration as determined by the Secretary of Defense." (U.S.C. 1970 ed.)

Table A-2. Increases in Cash Subsistence Allowances for Enlisted Personnel, Fiscal Years 1968–74

Date of adjustment	Daily rate (dollars)[a]	Percentage increase over preceding rate
October 1, 1967	1.31	9.6
July 1, 1968	1.33	1.4
January 1, 1970	1.39	4.7
January 1, 1971	1.52	9.4
January 1, 1972	1.46	−3.9
January 1, 1973	1.65	13.0
January 1, 1974	2.28	38.0

Source: Data provided by Department of Defense, Assistant Secretary of Defense for Manpower and Reserve Affairs, January 1974.
a. The subsistence rates shown are those paid to enlisted personnel who had access to government-furnished meals but who were given a choice of where to eat. When they did use government dining facilities, they were charged at a rate equal to their allowances, and the Defense Department bore the cost of preparing and serving the meals. Where government facilities were not available (for example, to recruiters in metropolitan areas), the daily subsistence rates were somewhat larger.

lowance . . . for all personnel, *the first such increase since 1963*."[3] In conference, the Senate receded, and quarters allowances were increased on an average by 47 percent for officers and approximately 31 percent for enlisted personnel.

Elements Influenced by Basic Pay

Under the Rivers method of calculating military comparability increases, other elements of compensation, not included in RMC but denominated in terms of basic pay, were increased more, proportionately, than was civilian pay. These elements—called "drag alongs"—include reservist drill pay, reenlistment bonuses, separation pay, government contributions to social security benefits, death gratuities, and continuation pay for physicians and dentists. Each increased with an increase in basic pay. At issue is the appropriateness of providing annual increases in, say, reservist drill pay that include a component intended as an increase in allowances, when the allowances themselves were not granted to reserve personnel. All together, these pay elements totaled about $3 billion in the budget for fiscal year 1974, a figure that would have been nearly $700 million less if increases for allowances had not been reflected in basic pay since 1968.

3. *Extension and Revision of the Draft Act and Related Laws,* H. Rept. 92-433, 92 Cong. 1 sess. (1971), p. 22. Italics added.

Also, since annuities for retired military personnel are computed as a percentage of basic pay, the formula has resulted in retired pay costs that are higher than they otherwise would be. Stated simply, the annuities of those personnel who retired since 1968 reflect increases in quarters and subsistence allowances and the tax advantage, as well as the rise in basic pay.

The succession of increases under this formula since 1968 has contributed to the ever-widening disparity between the annuities of those who retired before and those who retired after 1968. By today's standards, payments to pre-1968 retirees appear extremely low, resulting in pressures to increase them. For example, a lieutenant colonel who retired in January 1968 after having served twenty-two years received retired pay at that time amounting to $7,393 a year (55 percent of his basic pay at retirement). By January 1975, that annuity would have grown to about $11,411 as a result of annual adjustments based on the consumer price index. On the other hand, an officer of the same grade retiring with a similar period of service in January 1975 collects about $13,438 annually. Much of this difference of about 18 percent is due to the practice of including implicit increases in allowances and tax advantage in comparability adjustments to basic pay rates.